Psychology Revivals

Youth and Sex

Originally published in 1932, *Youth and Sex* was a book for those who wished to keep abreast of modern thought. A short review of the psychology of childhood and adolescence from a modern standpoint forms the core of the book. A preliminary section deals with the ethical and social problems of the day in relation to education, and with the conflict between the old generation and the new, while the concluding chapters review such questions as "The Girl and Her Education", "Sex Instruction", "The Marriage Question", etc. An up-to-date bibliography put the reader in touch with the best recent literature of the time. Today it can be read in its historical context.

This book is a re-issue originally published in 1932. The language used and views portrayed are a reflection of its era and no offence is meant by the Publishers to any reader by this re-publication.

Youth and Sex

A Psychological Study

Meyrick Booth

Routledge
Taylor & Francis Group
LONDON AND NEW YORK

First published in 1932
by George Allen & Unwin Ltd

This edition first published in 2026 by Routledge
4 Park Square, Milton Park, Abingdon, Oxon, OX14 4RN

and by Routledge
605 Third Avenue, New York, NY 10158

Routledge is an imprint of the Taylor & Francis Group, an informa business

Publisher's Note
The publisher has gone to great lengths to ensure the quality of this reprint but points out that some imperfections in the original copies may be apparent.

Disclaimer
The publisher has made every effort to trace copyright holders and welcomes correspondence from those they have been unable to contact.

For Product Safety Concerns and Information please contact our EU representative GPSR@taylorandfrancis.com. Taylor & Francis Verlag GmbH, Kaufingerstraße 24, 80331 München, Germany

A Library of Congress record exists under LCCN: 33001550

ISBN: 978-1-041-31871-2 (hbk)
ISBN: 978-1-003-78117-2 (ebk)
ISBN: 978-1-041-31890-3 (pbk)

Book DOI 10.4324/9781003781172

YOUTH AND SEX

A PSYCHOLOGICAL STUDY

by

MEYRICK BOOTH

B.Sc., Ph.D.

LONDON

GEORGE ALLEN & UNWIN LTD

MUSEUM STREET

FIRST PUBLISHED IN 1932,

PRINTED IN GREAT BRITAIN BY
UNWIN BROTHERS LTD., WOKING

TO

MY WIFE

CONTENTS

PART I

THE MODERN BACKGROUND

PART II

THE PSYCHOLOGY OF YOUTH

PART III

SPECIAL PROBLEMS

PART I

THE MODERN BACKGROUND

CHAPTER I

THE WORLD IN TRANSITION

a. ANTI-VICTORIANISM

It is, to-day, impossible to approach the problems of Youth and Sex along the lines which thirty, or even twenty, years ago would have seemed convincing.

The troubles and conflicts of society cannot be separated from those of the individual. The boy or girl of to-day cannot be isolated from the world-shaking movements of present-day life.

When universally accepted values, in social life and morals, constituted a rigid framework, within which youth quietly grew to maturity, we lived in a simpler and easier world.

The whole of western life has now become insecure and problematical.

We find ourselves in the midst of a vast movement of disintegration and transition. All accepted standards are challenged.

Any approach to the basic psychological questions with which this book is concerned is, in my opinion, *unreal* and misleading, which does not fully take into account not only the personal and individual factors but also the epoch-making social and ethical movements which now complicate the entire situation.

It is impossible for the educator to evade the special problems created by the confused situation of to-day. Sooner or later the attempt to make use of mere phrases will be found out. In a recent educational work, for example, I read that "young people should be taught respect for the moral law." But what is "the moral law" to the young man or woman of the modern great city?

Nothing could be more illusory than the idea that the chaos in the world of moral values can be concealed from the young. They are intuitively aware of it long before they grasp it intellectually.

To a demand to respect "the moral law" the modern emancipated adolescent says, "Yes, but do you mean the law of Christianity, the law of Nietzsche, the law of Bernard Shaw, the law of the cinema stage, the law of my office or factory mates, the law of the business world, the law of communism, or the law of individualism?"

In a society such as that of Victorian England, when Christian values were not challenged, even by non-Christians (save in very rare instances, which did not come to the notice of youth), we possessed a moral standard which offered youth a clearly defined goal. To-day, when a dozen conflicting conceptions of morality hold the field (and will be forced upon the boy or girl the moment they read fiction or visit the theatre), we can no longer fall back upon phrases like "the moral law." The truth is that comparatively few people realise the full extent of the revolution in fundamentals that has taken place in England during the last few years. From a nation composed of a large majority of Christians (if very imperfect ones!) we have become a people in which (perhaps) scarcely 25 per cent of the population can be reckoned as more than nominally Christian.

The Victorians, even when they attacked Christianity, believed firmly in the family and monogamy. So deeply rooted were their moral convictions that they did not even enter the area of questioning.

Now, however, the whole subject of sexual ethics has been thrown into the melting-pot. In every other novel written by a man, and in fully three-quarters of those written by women, the institution of marriage is challenged. In the course of a very extensive perusal of periodical literature I find it a rare event to come across any article dealing with marriage which is not more or less definitely anti-monogamous (if we except those written by Catholics).

No proposal is too fantastic to find favour with the modern reading public. A well-known young woman journalist suggests the legalisation of concubinage in England, and her ideas are quite well received. The fear of being thought "Victorian" seems to be extraordinarily effective in preventing any adverse criticism of the most revolutionary sexual proposals. If fifty years ago it was the correct thing to be orthodox, to-day those who do not hold "advanced" views on moral questions are soon made to feel that they are back-numbers. *Man muss mitmachen!*

The modern world is full of people so desperately afraid of being regarded as "out-of-date" that they will agree to accept almost any sort of conduct or opinion that is sufficiently far removed from the standards which they associate with horsehair sofas and the Albert Memorial. We have, in fact, to-day *a new cant*—the cant of *emancipation*. At all costs one must not run the terrible risk of being thought respectable and Victorian.

The other day a perfectly blameless and domesticated

young woman related to an old lady friend of mine, born in the fifties of last century, a tale about a man acquaintance of hers who invited his wife's sister to stay with him, and after a few weeks had sex relations with her, resulting in the birth of a baby. The old lady, not, I think, without some reason, expressed indignation, and met with the rebuke, "Well, you *are* a Victorian!" This was in quite ordinary English middle-class circles—in Yorkshire, to be precise.

b. THE REVOLT AGAINST MONOGAMY

The revolt against monogamy and the family—in fact against the whole Christian ethic in sex matters—is by no means (as is often supposed by the ill-informed) an affair of little cliques, of Bohemians, dwellers in Chelsea or Greenwich Village, N.Y. It now permeates (in very varying degrees) almost the entire community, having filtered downwards (or been absorbed upwards) from the *intelligentsia* who have for some time been its main propagandists. We must not forget that almost all writers of importance in England during the last thirty years have used their influence to undermine the family. Is it supposed that no result has been produced upon the mind of the nation? It would be a very strange situation if there were no relationship between the literature of a period and the actual state of feeling in the country producing the literature.

Those who are acquainted, at first hand, with the conditions obtaining in the England of to-day know that the sentiments of "the new morality" are heard, not only in the "advanced" circles of London, but just as frequently from the lips of factory girls, young engineers, or shop-assistants in Lancashire and Yorkshire or the Midlands.

The true significance of this revolt, to the parent and educator, is very far indeed from being adequately realised. *It is a central factor in the modern problem of Youth and Sex.*

We shall see later what a vital rôle in the development of youth is played by the *Zeitgeist*—even when those subjected to its all-pervading influence are too young to form intellectual impressions of a definite nature.

The temperamental optimism of the English, their notorious unwillingness to look awkward and unwelcome facts in the face, is probably, more than anything else, responsible for the general refusal to acknowledge the real importance of this revolt. We shrink from the idea that the comfortable security of Victorian morals is no longer existent for our children, and shelter behind soothing phrases—"a passing reaction," "those horrid novelists," and the like.

When Mr. Montgomery Belgion, in his illuminating book, *Our Present Philosophy of Life*, declared that the revolutionary sexual life-outlook of a Shaw, a Russell, or a Gide was to-day far more influential than the teaching of the Churches, some of his critics attempted to answer him with the childish objection that if a poll was taken in England the views mentioned by him would meet with very scanty support. This may be true. But is it seriously supposed that this is a *numerical* question? Let such a poll be taken not amongst the mass of the people but amongst novelists, dramatists, poets, artists, and reviewers—in short, where formative forces are at work—and who would venture to say that these views would receive only a small proportion of the votes?

Is it possible for any intelligent person to argue that the impingement upon the mind of the adolescent of a constant stream of suggestion, running directly contrary to all that he has (in most cases) been taught as to sexual matters at home and at school, can be without a deep influence upon his development?

Jack has been told at home, at school, and in church or chapel, that boys and girls should lead "pure lives," or in other words refrain from having sexual intercourse before marriage. At the age of, say, seventeen (or earlier) he begins to read for himself and to go to the theatre and cinema. He at once meets the view that chastity is "out-of-date," "Victorian," "injurious to health," and so forth, and he is told, either directly or indirectly, that temporary sex unions are not only "modern," but indeed essential to his health and moral development.[1]

It may be said he will not necessarily accept the views thus put before him. But even if he does not, the important fact is that *his life-outlook is rendered insecure*. He now realises that there are different opinions on these vital matters, and his confidence in a simple "right and wrong" is shattered. Those who are in touch with youth

[1] To take a real example: Ethel B., aged seventeen, who is being carefully educated according to Church of England ideas at great expense to her parents, is at home for the holidays; on the library table she picks up the current issue of one of our best-known literary weeklies and reads a middle-article by one of the most prominent of English women writers, arguing that no girl should marry without previously obtaining sexual experience (with the aid of birth control) from one, or more, of her boy friends. What is Ethel to think on reading these views in a journal which she knows to command the respect of her parents? I am not suggesting that the Press ought to be made safe for youth—far from it; I am merely pointing out, for the benefit of those who still wear blinkers, that a state of things now exists which immeasurably confuses the whole problem of sex and education.

know that what I say is true. Jack grows up doubting and questioning. Although the older generation may find it hard to believe it, tens of thousands of our best boys and girls, now passing through the most critical period of their lives, have entirely lost all bearings in a moral sense: this applies even to those who come from homes where the traditional values are respected.

A few months ago a case was brought to my notice of a young university woman student who said to one of her tutors, with whom she was on friendly terms: "Do you think I ought to have sex intercourse with boy friends? Many of my friends do it, and they tell me I ought to, for the sake of the experience. I feel so puzzled as to what is right." Such a question as this, which was asked in good faith, throws a vivid light on the vastly changed conditions of life in England since the war.

The difficulties of the situation are added to by the fact that a large proportion of the older generation still keep their heads firmly buried in the sand, and refuse entirely to aid those who (like myself) are seeking to clarify the situation and bring some order into the chaos. These ostriches, perceiving no problem, cannot understand what all the fuss is about. The Bishop of London, who referred to the dangers of "companionate marriage" in a speech made while I was writing this chapter, was at once attacked by a leading London daily on the ground that his fears were imaginary, and that our young unmarried people (so it was implied) all lived chaste lives! It is this type of obstinate refusal to face plain facts that causes an acute foreign observer, M. André Siegfried, to speak of our "vague, indolent method of setting aside realities" and our unwillingness even to formulate problems, let alone solve them! (*England's Crisis*, p. 141.)

The present refusal (in wide circles) to recognise the existence of a moral crisis is on a par with the blindness of the great mass of the nation to the economic crisis prior to September 1931.

. . . . .

If it be said that I devote too much space to an aspect of modern life that is not directly related to the theme of this study, I reply that there is no hard-and-fast line between individual and social psychology. The young human does not grow up in a vacuum. He is, from the beginning, a member of a certain society. The various intellectual and atmospheric influences of this society surround him from birth. His attitude towards sex can never be a purely individual matter.

It is therefore essential to examine, however briefly, the nature of the moral background before taking up the more intimately psychological problems of Chapters IV to VII. For it will there be seen clearly that the critical problems of adolescence are completely bound up with the structure and standards of the community, and cannot be truly analysed without regard to ultimate values.[1]

Even should a given group hold itself aloof from the life around it and maintain a religious and moral existence of its own (as amongst Quakers or strict Catholics), it

[1] Dr. Hans Richert writes in his very excellent little book, *Psychologie und Pädagogik der Entwicklungsjahre* (p. 27): "Who could deny . . . that the protective power of morality, the lighthouse of eternal, universally valid and all-dominating convictions—forces making for health—has grown weaker? The disintegrated *Kultur* of to-day has filled life with problems, and these invade the soul of the adolescent along a thousand different avenues. To-day, he is provided with a formula of justification for every forbidden pleasure."

cannot escape the specific influences of the age; for the mere fact that a life cut off, in many respects, from that of the community at large is being lived by the group will itself influence the development of the young, producing a tension which may deeply affect the psychic integration of the youth of the group.

In Dr. Hadfield's informative book, *Psychology and Morals*, we have, in the early chapters, a very lucid exposition of human development as a movement towards completion, a search after *wholeness*. This is in fact the keynote of the psychology of youth—a growth of the immature towards maturity, a process of fulfilment.

But this *becoming whole* cannot be conceived of as an isolated process. If the mind of the community, on its higher levels of thought, is split into warring sections, this lack of wholeness in the larger life is reflected in the mind of the child and adolescent and powerfully works against its growth towards completion as a unified whole.

c. THE SOUTH SEA PARADISE

In his contribution, "After the Family—What?" (*The New Generation*, p. 55 (Allen & Unwin), the well-known American psychologist, Dr. J. B. Watson, sums up the characteristics of the new ethic which (in his opinion) is now conquering the mind of youth: there will be a large freedom for sexual experimentation amongst adolescents (after the fashion of primitive tribes); young men will find "by trial and error" which girl gives them the largest amount of sexual satisfaction. To make this freedom possible there must be a perfect scientific control of conception, an improvement in the means of avoiding venereal infection, and a facilitation of abortion (Dr.

Watson thinks it would be advisable for the State hospitals to agree to examine any couple contemplating a sexual experiment and provide a certificate of health, as part of the campaign for stamping out sexual diseases). We must drop every idea of sin or of moral obligation, couples being as free as air to unite and separate; the ensuing mating (should one occur of a more permanent nature) will, in the author's opinion, be much more successful than the marriage of to-day, since it will be between a young man and a young woman both of whom have had experience of sex intercourse with equals prior to choosing each other. Should children be born, these can, if desired, be cared for in a State nursery.

At this stage I can comment only very briefly on the extraordinary lack of psychological insight displayed by this professor of psychology. Does he, for example, really suppose that civilised couples can come together and then part as free as air, as if they were dogs or cats (save that the cat takes a much greater interest in her offspring than Dr. Watson seems to expect from his young women)? What of the cases, which would be very numerous, when the man came to the conclusion, after conducting an "experiment" (with due assistance from the hospital), that his girl friend did not suit him, but the poor girl thought otherwise, and became passionately attached to him? We all know how often this (or the reverse process) does actually happen in modern free relationships. There is not the barest hint in this professorial vision of a sexual New Jerusalem of the depths and complications which the sex problem presents to beings who, by virtue of their entire structure, mental and physical, are *not* cats or dogs!

This outline of "the new morality" is very instructive.

In the first place, it shows us how "advanced" tendencies, when allowed free play, lead logically to the reduction of man to a level rather lower than that of the more intelligent animals. Further, it is of special interest because (improbable as this may seem to those who hide their heads in the sand) it is *thoroughly typical*. The eminent behaviourist is only one of ten thousand intellectuals holding closely similar ideals now working busily to influence the mind of youth. Let us hear what one of the leading mentors of English youth—Lord (better known as Bertrand) Russell—has to say on the same topic:

"My own view is that the State and the law should take no notice of sexual relations apart from children, and that no marriage ceremony should be valid unless accompanied by a medical certificate of the woman's pregnancy. But when once there are children, I think that divorce should be avoided except for a very grave cause. I should not regard physical infidelity as a very grave cause, and should teach people that it is to be expected and tolerated, but should not involve the begetting of illegitimate children. . . ." (Quoted in *Sex and Civilisation*, p. 427.)

Mr. Calverton writes (*The Bankruptcy of Marriage*, p. 308): "The attitude now dominant in Soviet Russia, which regards sex relations as a matter entirely private and personal, with neither State nor convention as supervisor, is the attitude that is rapidly becoming accepted in practice, if not in theory, by the rest of the world."[1]

. . . . .

[1] It is a great error to suppose that the revolt against monogamy is confined to those outside the Churches. I was recently present at a discussion between a supporter of monogamy and the headmistress

It would be easy for me to multiply such quotations almost *ad lib*. In its essence, the modern situation (as envisaged by the interpreters of the new sexual freedom) is a *reversion* to the conditions obtaining in very primitive communities—such as the dwellers in the Trobriand Isles, so closely investigated by Malinowski. The "modern" dreams of a new paganism, from which all the restraints and disciplines of religion and morality have been banished for ever, and we are all free to live the life of the flesh, with the happy innocence of the South Seas or the sinless animals. (It is not, of course, so much the conditions *actually* obtaining in these communities which are here in mind as those which are *supposed* to obtain by those who do not know much about primitive life; nothing could be further from the mind of the pseudo-South Sea islander than the system of taboos really existing in the Pacific. Cf. also p. 198.)

of a girls' school (herself a Church member), which ran on the following lines:

SUPPORTER OF MONOGAMY. Am I right in assuming that you support marriage?

HEADMISTRESS. Certainly I do.

S.M. You believe in Christian marriage?

H.M. Yes.

S.M. Supposing a couple have been married for some time and they find their affection is cooling down, what should they do?

H.M. They ought to separate.

S.M. And live single lives?

H.M. No, certainly not, that is unnatural.

S.M. You mean they should find fresh partners?

H.M. Of course.

S.M. You do not think that runs contrary to Christian teaching?

H.M. No, because Christ taught that marriage should be based on love; a marriage without love is sin.

S.M. You think that a man or woman might in this way make quite a series of experiments in sexual union?

H.M. (*rather unwillingly*). Well, I suppose that can't be helped.

All this to the average member of the respectable middle-class will seem terribly shocking. But I confess that I entirely refuse to be shocked. What we here encounter is not in any sense "wicked" or "daring." It is best described by the term *childish*. A person must be very innocent indeed, and very inexperienced in realities, to be capable of assuming that the mere liberation of the sex impulse will make us all happy. One is irresistibly reminded here of what I may call the "sugar-toffee mentality." When Tommy is four or five years of age he is quite certain that if he only had an unlimited supply of toffee, he would be permanently blissful. Let him have it, and in an hour or two he will be violently ill. And to-day, in those circles where sexual freedom has been, for some little while, the fashion, we already discern very distinct signs of nausea.

Life is not so simple as all this. The psyche of the educated European is far too complicated for a mere reversion to pagan freedom to satisfy its cravings. An instinct for form and order is part of the inherited equipment of the higher races, and quite apart from any theological or Puritanical considerations, the disintegration of moral and social life accompanying this reversion will not in the long run prove tolerable.

Professor W. McDougall does well to remind us that the Trobriand Islanders are not, after all, a creative race; and that it was Dante who wrote immortal poetry and not Casanova.

Later some further aspects of this problem will be considered (see Chapter XII). I must here remark, in passing, that those sections of modern opinion which take up what I may call the South Sea attitude towards the sex problem can make no claim to be *objective*.

Their conclusions and opinions are usually determined by reversed taboos. In other words, they simply take the Christian position on any given question and turn it upside-down. It is often, indeed, quite amusing, in reading a symposium like *The New Generation* (cf. p. 193), to perceive how one writer after another automatically denounces everything which orthodox religion finds good, and praises everything which the Churches denounce!

The "freedom" of this school does not, in actual practice, amount to anything more than an inward compulsion always to reach a goal the precise opposite of that aimed at by the religiously orthodox.

How far this is due to subconscious bias and how far to an instinct for self-advertisement ("Oh, my dear, you positively *must* read Miss X's new book—so daring, so outspoken, so *naughty*!") I cannot pretend to say. But it is quite absurd to suppose that a genuine thinker would invariably arrive at an anti-Christian end-point. A religion that has held sway over so many millions of the highest races for so long must contain *something* of truth.

Quite otherwise is the situation where we find real originality and independence. Four of the most acute minds of to-day, Aldous Huxley, Wyndham Lewis, Count Keyserling, and Waldo Frank, have all arrived by processes of pure thought at positions which make the blind and essentially emotional and immature anti-traditional reaction look a very cheap affair indeed. And these positions do not represent adherence to orthodoxy but an advance to a wider conception of reality than could be perceived within the outlook of a mere *anti*-movement.

d. CHAOS

The reversion to the primitive (which is the really characteristic feature of nearly all present-day tendencies in the field of sex) does not supply us with a new system of morality. It is not, in practice, possible for the ethics of the South Seas to be transplanted to British soil and there take firm root. What really happens is simply that the new individualistic ideas of freedom in matters of sex act as an acid, corroding the framework of our society. We obtain no basis upon which to build. "Retrogression is not the future," wrote D. H. Lawrence. "Fifty million children growing up purposeless, with no purpose save the attainment of their own individual desires, these are not the future; they are only a disintegration of the past. The future is living, growing truth, in advancing fulfilment" (*Twilight in Italy*, part ii).

In the various credos put forward by "moderns"—I believe in kindness, I believe in tolerance, I believe in being "civilised," and so forth—there is nothing constructive, since all such standards are purely subjective; they possess no formative power whatever.

. . . . .

A very common misunderstanding of the present situation is revealed in the use of such phrases as "the conflict between the old morality and the new morality." There is no such thing as "a new morality" in any real sense of the term. The essence of what is so-called is simply the individualisation of sex, the proclamation of freedom from *any* law. There may be almost as many suggestions for reformed moralities as there are reformers;

but none of these has any authority. No clear-cut "new morality" holds the field as an alternative to traditional morality. In the modern mood this would scarcely be possible, for, as Mr. Julien Benda says, nothing is so characteristic of the modern mind as its dislike of definition, its preference for all that is vague, indistinct, and chaotic.

From the standpoint of the parent and educator this is a more difficult situation than that which would result from a triumph of actual South Sea islanders. For in the Pacific there are certain well-defined taboos and customs which create an ethic of sorts. But what we have to face in the western world to-day is a state of confusion and disintegration in which large sections of young people, not yet ripe for autonomy, grow up without any guiding, directing influence.

The idea, held widely enough to-day, that the disintegration of definite values leaves the way open for an unfettered development of youth is, psychologically speaking, utterly erroneous. It is here assumed that the developing adolescent is *an entirely ego-centric* being, evolving his life from within alone. The deeply significant matter of *the formative influence of socially sanctioned truths and values* upon the evolving mind of youth is simply ignored. In reality the movement towards maturity, of which we have spoken (p. 23), tends to be arrested when the expanding organism fails (as is now often the case) to find a link with the larger whole. For the reactions which should take place between the unit and the whole are a part of the process through which the former achieves its own individual wholeness. The integration of the unit is not a problem which can be solved in divorce from life as a whole.

e. THE NEED FOR A POSITIVE ETHIC

If we resolve to go beyond a superficial view of the problem of Youth and Sex we cannot avoid facing ultimate ethical and philosophical problems.

There is in reality no such thing as education without a life-philosophy. In *The Philosophical Bases of Education* Dr. Rusk writes, "From every angle of the educational problem comes thus the demand for a philosophical basis of the subject. There is no escape from a philosophy of life and of education. Those who pride themselves on their neglect of philosophy have their own philosophy —usually a quite inadequate one—" (p. 22); and again, "Teachers who assume that they can afford to ignore philosophy pay the penalty of their neglect, for their efforts, lacking a co-ordinating principle, are thereby rendered ineffective" (p. 20).

If this is true of education in general, it is quite especially true of the sexual aspect of the teacher's or parent's task. For there is a far closer bond between sex and life than between (say) arithmetic or geography and life.

As Dr. Rusk points out, the naturalistic tendency is now strongly in the ascendant in the world of education (especially in England and America), and if we take up this position (leaving ultimate problems on one side as being too "metaphysical") we shall sooner or later find ourselves led into a very awkward position—unless we are prepared to be "naturalists" in the fullest sense of the term, and to repudiate our traditional morality entirely.

Suppose, for example, we start sex instruction with plants and then, as is now so often done, go on to animals (drawing the usual analogy between the animal world and the human in order to explain the facts of sex life), the more intelligent pupils will be apt to view the whole problem of sex from the animal standpoint, to think: "Sex intercourse amongst animals is more or less promiscuous; we are—as we have seen in these lessons—higher animals; why should not we, too, practise sexual promiscuity?" If any effective answer is to be given to this very pertinent question the teacher must have behind him some definite philosophy of sex; he must be able to relate sex in some convincing way to our moral and social life. To treat sex in matter-of-fact style, as if it were a branch of natural history and nothing more, is to tread what is—from the standpoint of those who are not prepared to throw morality overboard—a very dangerous path indeed.

When the teacher or parent stands upon a positive basis, and the sex education can thus be related to a view of life as a whole—as in Catholic or definitely Protestant Christian homes and schools—the problem of approach is simpler (although, in this case too, there remains the difficult question of the contradiction which may, and probably will, arise between the ideals of the school or home and those of the outside world, see p. 117). But when, as is now frequently the case, those responsible for the education of the child do not themselves occupy any clear position in regard to the sex question, although desirous of saving their charges from the perils of sex, the problem of sex instruction becomes almost insoluble.

. . . . .

The tendency of modern thought in general and of the educational system in particular will incline the parent or teacher to the naturalistic-biological approach, which, if pursued at all logically (and children are apt to be embarrassingly logical!), must lead to the natural (or animal) ideal of sex morality—the gratification of the sex instinct whenever the inclination or temptation arises. If another ideal is introduced—such as that of monogamy and chastity before marriage—it is unrelated to the original method of approach and will therefore not appeal to the boys and girls with the same force; it will not form a part of the instruction as a whole, and will be apt to seem "dragged in."

The fact is that the Christian ethic still exerts an enormous (if vague and sentimental) influence over multitudes of men and women who have long since ceased to be believers. There are to-day hundreds of thousands of English parents who could not conscientiously teach their children from the religious standpoint, but who would draw the line at accepting the logical implications of the modern naturalistic sex-outlook and teaching their children that it is right and normal for them to enjoy sexual intercourse when and with whom they like. In other words, such parents wish to safeguard the family, although they have ceased to hold the religious and ethical views which are the basis of the family system.

At this point we find ourselves in one of the fighting trenches on that immense battle-front which now divides the forces of Christian tradition, centring upon Rome, from the hosts of organised materialistic communism whose capital is Moscow. The one side in this world-wide struggle (the full import of which is only just beginning to be glimpsed) stands for monogamy supported by religious sanctions, and the other proclaims the ethic of complete sexual freedom based upon the purely naturalistic view of man's nature and moral duties, which is the upshot of physical science as applied to the sex problem. However much the issue in any given sector may be complicated by cross-currents and confused by local circumstances, it is at bottom a phase of this world-conflict.

CHAPTER II

THE MODERN SPIRIT

a. THE MODERN SPIRIT
b. MODERN PSYCHOLOGY
c. "LIKE A PANIC!"

a. THE MODERN SPIRIT

In the western world the conflict is not — as in Russia — between tradition and a definite system of materialism.

The modern Englishman or American does not argue about religion. He does not oppose it with the fiery zeal of a Bradlaugh, a French atheist, or a Russian communist. He ignores it entirely. The whole controversy is to him unimportant and unreal.

It may be true that in certain thoughtful circles there is still much discussion of spiritual and moral questions. But amongst the crowds of young men and their girl friends who flock to the cinema and the football-ground there are very few indeed to whom religion means anything. And if we are to believe Mr. Joad, who has devoted much care to the study of the religious outlook of youth, the great majority of university students are entirely devoid of any interest in religion. To them it belongs to a past age, and they regard with mild amusement the efforts of those who seek to interest them in anything so fossilised.

In his work, *The Present and Future of Religion*, Mr. Joad goes so far as to say: "For the first time in history there is coming to maturity a generation of men and women who have no religion and feel no need for one."[1]

The chief factor in the modern western world (as distinct from Russia) is not any definable form of atheism or materialism. It is a much vaguer and more elusive thing. Mr. Joad calls it "the modern spirit." Mr. Montgomery Belgion, in his recent work with that title, calls it "Our Present Philosophy of Life."

It is not a system of beliefs alternative to Christianity; it is rather the state of mind of possessing no beliefs.

It is a special sort of attitude towards life, and not a creed. Self-expression is its watchword. All definite ethical standards are repudiated in the interests of a subjective life-outlook. The individual is made the measure of all things, as in the days of Athenian sophistry. "Reality is reduced to ashes," in the phrase of Alfred Noyes. The sophist Pyrrho was the real prototype of the modern thinker. He said: "Nothing should be denied; nothing should be affirmed. Or if one of the two seems necessary, let the affirmation and the denial be concurrent."[2]

There is nothing in common between the modern

The well-known Roman Catholic, Father Woodlock, who has a very wide knowledge of London life, recently expressed the view that young people of all classes now grow up in the belief that "Christianity has been exploded as a fallacy," and he added that the average public schoolboy is "a very charming pagan."

[2] An example, at once characteristic and amusing, of our twentieth-century sophistry is to be seen in the oft-repeated modern argument against the traditional ethic of monogamy: this restriction (it is said) has stunted the sex life and caused untold harm through repression; but side by side with this statement is almost always to be found a charge of exactly the opposite nature, namely that orthodox morals have never been anything but hypocrisy, that in reality Christians have all along lived polygamously, while merely professing monogamy. In this case, where was the harmful repression?

outlook and what used to be called rationalism. To-day reason is at least as unpopular as religion.

The influence of the great anti-rationalists—such as Nietzsche, Shaw, Freud, Proust, W. James, Bergson,[1] Sorel, and Berth (with his "let us go back to the sub-conscious")—spreads far beyond the ranks of students and writers and now subtly affects the life-outlook of the masses.

It is a special feature of our age that its intellectual leaders are anti-intellectualists. They have, in effect, ceased to reason and become the apostles of various forms of irrationalism—such as intuitionism, vitalism, instinctivism, futurism, primitivism, and emotional naturalism.

We may fairly hold our "feelers" (a term which I am sure they will prefer to "thinkers") largely responsible for the characteristically amorphous quality of modern mental life.

As Keyserling observes in *Creative Understanding*, the soul-life of the typical modern has no definable structure; it is amorphous and wholly devoid of the rigidity necessary in order to resist environmental influences; hence "things rule over persons."[2]

[1] Cf. *The Art of Being Ruled* (Wyndham Lewis): "Bergson . . . has been the great organiser of disintegration in the modern world: it is he who has found all the reasons . . . for the destruction of the things of the intellect and the handing over to sensation of the privileges and heirlooms of the mind . . ." (p. 386). "The root impulse in Bergson's philosophy was a rendering back to *life*, magiscular abstraction of a feverish chaos, all that the mind had taken from her to build into forms and concepts" (p. 389).

[2] Cf. also Christopher Dawson's *Christianity and the New Age*, p. 18: "In the period since the war there has been a growing tendency towards the de-intellectualisation and exteriorisation of European life. The old fixed canons of social and moral conduct have been abandoned, and society has given itself up to the current of external change

Nothing irritates your real modern so much (says M. Benda in his penetrating study *Belphegor*) as order, discipline, authority, or mental consistency—in fact, anything giving *form* to mind or society. All must be intangible, flowing, relative, subjective, and indefinable. "An organically disordered world" is his ideal. General ideas are anathema. Artists and "feelers" must concern themselves only with the particular. The extraordinary influence of Joyce's *Ulysses* is due to the fact that it perfectly reflects this mood.

Obviously, to discuss the genesis of the present-day spirit would take us too far afield. But, in passing, the following causes are suggested: the decline of traditional religion; the attack upon reason and the progress of instinct psychology; relativism in science; the subjection of man to nature, resulting from the scientific outlook and the consequent loss of will and inner freedom; the more external limitations of freedom following upon the ever-increasing power of the state; and, finally, the purely nervous and physical effect of the speed and restlessness of modern life—a factor by no means to be underrated. To all these we must add the shattering effect of the Great War.

. . . . .

While thus emphasising the great significance of the

without any attempt towards self-direction or the preservation of spiritual continuity," and on p. 16 we read that man, through the growth of science, "gradually loses his position of exception and superiority, and sinks back into nature," becoming "a subordinate part of the great mechanical system," while the application of science to economic and practical life "ends in the subjection of man to the rule of the machine," and in the field of politics to the "absolutism of the modern national state."

"modern spirit," it would be a mistake to overestimate the rôle which it plays in the modern scene.

The Churches are very far from being so "played out" as the often over-confident modern supposes them to be. If numerically weaker, they still command a following influential enough to resist with success almost all the more revolutionary proposals of the moral left-wing.[1]

Supposing, to take an example, that the proposals of the advanced feminists to legalise "trial marriage" in England were actually to be introduced into Parliament in the form of a definite Bill: does anyone imagine for a moment that it would stand any chance of success?

In an actual positive sense the moral revolutionaries are still very weak as compared with the more orthodox sections of the community. Their strength lies, however, in the solvent influence of their ideas. They are not strong enough to prevail, but they are able to create a general atmosphere of doubt and insecurity which, if it does not secure their own victory, at any rate paralyses their opponents.

The result is a deadlock. Neither side in the conflict can force a victory, or is at all likely to do so within measurable time. We are thus left with no generally accepted ideals and no unquestioned standards.

[1] The mere fact that amongst Roman Catholics the birth-rate is more than 50 per cent higher than it is amongst non-Catholics seems to indicate that the future may hold surprises in store for those who reckon confidently on a rapid decay of all the religious bodies. Nothing is more characteristic of the moderns than their extreme reluctance to bring children into the world. This being the case, it is more than possible (as Benjamin Kidd envisaged) that the numerical decline of those races or sections of society holding these views may lead to the triumph of the life-outlook of other and more prolific races and sections. The conflict may be decided in the nursery rather than in the study or laboratory!

b. MODERN PSYCHOLOGY

One of the most significant developments of our time is the popularisation of a type of psychological teaching which reduces personality to instinct, with the virtual elimination of will and reason.

There can be no doubt that this tendency has been one of the most potent agents in the creation of our uncertainty and confusion. What room can there be for positive morality or indeed for any definite thinking or volition at all in a world governed (as we are told) wholly by obscure instincts?

The name of Freud, in particular, is associated with this teaching, but other schools of thought—such as the McDougallites[1] and the Adlerians—are hardly, if at all, less committed to instinctivism; while behaviourism (so influential in the United States and Russia) is the most extreme example conceivable of a psychology which leaves no room for will, intellect, or soul.

Keyserling writes: "What is the essence of behaviourism? That man is an animal like any other. That spiritual initiative and free-will play practically no part in his make-up and conduct—what he develops into is thought to be entirely a matter of natural stimulation, in about the same sense as the frog in the laboratory inevitably responds to specific stimuli in a specific way."

[1] "We may say then that directly or indirectly the instincts are the prime-movers of all human activity. . . . The instinctive impulses determine the ends of all activities and supply the driving power by which all mental activities are sustained; and all the complex intellectual apparatus of the most highly developed mind is but a means towards these ends, is but the instrument by which these impulses seek their satisfactions, while pleasure and pain do but serve to guide them in their choice of the means." (McDougall, *Social Psychology*, 2nd ed., p. 38.)

This reduction of man to the level of the animals is indeed the essence of the modern movement in psychology, especially as the movement is popularly understood. The qualification is of some importance, since there is no lack of exponents of the so-called new psychology who—perhaps rather illogically—would resist such an interpretation. But the fact remains that the impression left upon the mind of the public is that modern psychology has taught that instinct is supreme, and that will and independent intellectual and spiritual life are figments or at best a species of sublimation. And it is with this impression that we are now concerned.

It is thus possible for a popular writer like Mr. Blyton (*The Modern Adventure*, p. 40) to say with truth, "To-day the 'New Psychology' . . . is upsetting the idealism, faith, and even the self-respect of thousands of impressionable people."

Other psychologies, newer than the "New" Psychology —such as Personalism, the so-called *Geistes-psychologie* and *Gestalt* psychology—which, in different degrees, tend to counteract the above-described movement, are scarcely as yet known to the general public.

. . . . .

In the foregoing argument we have looked upon modern psychology as a *cause* of modern mentality. But the opposite possibility should not be overlooked. What if the mind of the age produces a psychology suitable to its mood? Plutocracy, mass-production, and routine-life—supposing them to give rise to a special sort of psychology—would undoubtedly produce something extremely like behaviourism. It is the ideal psychology from the standpoint of those who wish to see a docile population of efficient machine-minders and absorbers of officially engineered propaganda. We need not feel surprised that behaviourism has "caught on" in Russia. To the wire-pullers of the Kremlin it must seem like a gift from heaven. The warm advocacy of these doctrines on the part of numerous professors of psychology installed in the millionaire-endowed universities of the States is also easily understandable on grounds not purely scientific. (In *The Art of Being Ruled* and *Time and Western Man*, Mr. Wyndham Lewis has thrown out many brilliant suggestions with regard to the genesis of modern philosophy and psychology regarded in relation to modern politics and social life; and in spite of their difficulty these works richly repay careful study on the part of all who desire to dig below the surface of present-day social life.)[1]

Whatever the precise nature of the cause and effect relationships may be, we can safely place on record the close connection which exists between the "modern spirit" of emotionalism and intellectual vagueness, modern psychology, and the present-day purposelessness and drift in all matters social and political.

It is no objection to urge that numbers of leading personalities do not accept either the psychology or the mental moods to which we have referred. They are influenced in spite of themselves and without the knowledge of their own conscious selves. It is the decay of faith in personality and will, the passive reliance upon mechanical extra-human "processes" and "tendencies," which has paralysed the initiative and lamed the political energy of the whole of the western world.

[1] The reader is referred also to the work by Dr. Haas, mentioned on p. 58.

c. "LIKE A PANIC!"

In the field of sex the result of the factors briefly, and I am afraid very inadequately, indicated in the foregoing sections has been forcibly described by Mr. H. G. Wells (*The World of William Clissold*, book vi, part iii):

"The manners and morals, the laws and arrangements between the sexes to-day, the expectations people have and the rights they claim in love and marriage, constitute now a vast, dangerous, unhappy conflict and confusion. It has ceased to follow a code or a system. It is like a panic, like a *débâcle*. In the past there has been stress, suppression, and sorrow in sexual life, but never so chancy, unjust, and wasteful a time as this one. It is a state of affairs in which no one is safe for happiness, and no conduct sure of success. For most of us there is an obligation to blunder...."

It is the present mood of passivity, of will-less surrender to instinct, of essential *aimlessness*, which, more than anything else, gives rise to this "conflict and confusion." (It is, of course, true that there are millions of men and women who know and care nothing about this modern "conflict and confusion," who live still in the grooves of tradition, but I am here discussing those self-conscious and intellectually active circles who constitute "modern life" as distinct from those who live in the world of to-day, but are not of it.)

Most of the diatribes directed against "modern youth" by well-meaning parents, teachers, or ministers of religion are quite beside the mark. The emancipated new generation is in no sense immoral, vicious, or depraved; and it is not its fault if the dissolution of values resulting from modern developments in science, and thought in general, leaves it with no firm ground upon which to stand.

Such is not the *desire* of youth. Few things are really so striking in the life of to-day—to those who have the eyes to see it—as the revolt of youth against freedom. It is only in the view of those who belong, mentally, to the pre-war period that youth appears as a symbol of insurrection and libertarianism. The actual young man of to-day is not a disciple of Godwin, Shelley, or Swinburne!

In France, where the exceptional mental alertness of the people so often anticipates the movements of European social life, a new and deep moral earnestness on the part of young men and women of the student class is an outstanding fact. In Germany, the young generation has filled the ranks of such disciplined and, in English eyes, excessively authoritarian organisations as the Hitler movement and the *Stahlhelm*. This is due, in no small degree, to an impatient rejection of the gospel of aimless liberty which swept Germany in the years after the war, and the craving of youth for a life of order and *form*.

In England, as we can see very plainly, it is elderly men like Bernard Shaw and Lord Russell—whose mentality is deeply rooted in reactions dating from the Victorian age and in an iconoclasm which is to-day almost meaningless—who champion the cause of emancipation in the nineteenth-century tradition.

Where a movement springs *from* youth, as in the case of Italian Fascism or German National Socialism, the main emphasis is laid upon unity and discipline.

. . . . .

Thus modern youth finds itself torn in two—on the one hand it craves, subconsciously perhaps more than consciously, for a new meaning and form; on the other, it still, to some considerable extent, swims in the backwash of the anti-Victorian reaction.

Even when we consider those by no means negligible sections of youth which experiment, to the horror of the older generation—in so far as the latter will allow itself to perceive the situation—in various brands of sexual freedom, we should not forget that it is more a peculiar type of *innocence* that is responsible for their conduct than anything deliberately immoral. This statement will be accepted by those who have been in personal contact with such "cases," and have seen at close quarters the total inability to attach any meaning to orthodox views of "right" and "wrong" on the part of many modern emancipated young people.

A girl of seventeen or eighteen is not sufficiently mature to understand the deeper significance of sex life. She is often perfectly sincere when she argues: "If I like to spend the night with my best boy, how does that hurt anybody? I understand enough to make sure I shall not have a baby. We both have a good time, and nobody is any the worse for it!" To-day such arguments are put forward in the naïvest fashion. They reveal the essentially innocent crudity of the undeveloped mind of adolescence. What we here perceive is not anything "bad" in youth, but the breakdown of our culture, which has left a vacuum where there should have been inspiring life-ideals.

The wiping-out of boundaries and distinctions has left youth groping for a foothold, and often the prey of subconscious forces that it is totally unable to analyse.

It is here that the function of the adult comes in. It is the business of the parent and teacher (school, university, or religious) to interpret the world to youth and youth to itself. If masses of young people are to-day wandering pathless through life, it is the adults who are mainly responsible. After all, it is they and not the young people, who made this world of vagueness, chaos, and confusion into which the adolescent of to-day is thrust.

CHAPTER III

THE OLD GENERATION AND THE NEW

a. FATHERS AND SONS
b. YOUTH UPROOTED
c. FREEDOM AND AUTHORITY

a. FATHERS AND SONS

The very rapid growth—chiefly, of course, amongst the young—of what we may call a "modern" life-outlook has, for one of its most far-reaching results, the opening up of *an immense gulf between the older and younger generations*.

It may be argued by those who do not look below the surface that there has always been such a gulf, that the conflict of parent and child is a phenomenon common to human life in all ages.

That there has been from time immemorial a certain tension between the grown-ups and the growing-ups is true. This tension is indeed needful for the development of youth.

But the present situation is radically different from that of preceding ages.

To go back some fifty years. The tension between father and son in 1880 was personal. They were separated by the natural difference in psychological development. Where conflict existed, it was the age-long strife between immaturity and maturity. The basic beliefs of the older generation were not challenged on principle by the younger generation as is now often the case.

The adolescents were then engaged in claiming their place in a world which they *accepted*, and the struggle was to secure a place in that world. They were not "out" to destroy the world of their elders.

What lends such extraordinary intensity to the present-day conflict between the old and young is the clash of moral and spiritual values. The father is often engaged, consciously or unconsciously, in moulding his son to views which the latter inwardly repudiates, while the son is fighting for ideals which the father could not accept without turning his back upon his whole personality.[1]

In practice it often happens that the father or mother solves the problem in the easiest way—by an *abdication of responsibility*. They simply let the young people go their own way. A friendly relationship is kept up, but the older generation ceases to act educationally upon the younger. Outwardly, this solution not infrequently yields good results. Father and son are "good pals," but the maturity of the former ceases to act fruitfully upon the mind of the latter. In the long run the young generation suffers heavily from this abdication on the part of those who should perform a certain psychological function in the evolution of the immature (see p. 112, *note*). To place an overload of responsibility on the shoulders of the young may be to injure their psychic life seriously.

To-day, as we all know, there are countless homes in which the parents have taken their hands off the wheel. Young boys and girls, at an age when they cannot understand life, come and go at all hours of the day and night.

[1] This situation is seen, for example, in several of Galsworthy's novels, and in J. D. Beresford's trilogy, *Three Generations*.

They snatch a meal, sleep a few hours, and are off again. Frequently (even in the most respectable middle-class homes) sex connections are formed without the parents having the faintest notion of what is going on (this is no random statement, for it is based upon an exact knowledge of specific instances). Or the parents may know without daring, or caring, to intervene.

• • • • •

That the period of immaturity, during which the young should be in some degree of dependence, is longer the higher up we go in the evolutionary scale is an important biological truth. Hence this premature casting loose of their offspring by so many modern parents is a sign of *regression*. They simply abandon a cultural task to which they are not equal. It is a return to a lower and less highly evolved type of social and moral life.

The enormous importance of the parent-child relationship in a psychological sense is almost a discovery of our age. We now know that the nature of the bond between mother and son, father and daughter, is deeper and more fraught with significance for good or evil than had previously been imagined. This is perhaps the least disputable of all the conclusions of the new school of psychology.

There is a rather strange irony in the fact that the age which discovers quite a new depth and significance in the parent relationship is the same age in which, more than ever before, parental authority and responsibility are weakened. Never, it will be generally admitted, has the father had so little influence; and yet never before has the psychological and pedagogical importance of the father been so fully recognised on the theoretical side!

In passing, the reader will perceive that at this point two powerful influences meet in opposition. The stream of modern psychology here cuts right across the still strong (although weakening) current of nineteenth-century individualism, with its tendency to undermine the family and belittle parenthood. We glimpse distinctly a conflict destined shortly to play a large part in social life: namely, that between the atomism of the individualistic life-outlook (handed down to us from the last generation) and the newer organic outlook of social psychology.

. . . . .

The existence of this abnormally wide gulf between parent and adolescent child in the modern world, especially in the more intellectually awakened classes, has an important bearing upon the problem of Youth and Sex.

To-day, even when the parents are on friendly terms with the adolescent, they are apt to represent a point of view no longer acceptable to the younger generation. If fifty or sixty years ago the difficulty was that a young boy of (say) seventeen years was shy of talking to his father on more intimate subjects, to-day there is the more serious difficulty that, although well enough able to talk to his father, he may have little or no respect for his point of view.

A mere descent on the part of parents to the level of the immature, in an endeavour to become the companions and friends of their own children, is one of the commonest phenomena of the day. But what is this but another form of evasion? They do not, it is true, cast their children loose. But they seek to become children themselves.

In this way they cease, practically speaking, to give their children anything more than they can get just as well from other children. This is, in essence, only another kind of abandonment of the parent-child relationship, with all that it should mean for the development of the child.

The parents' business is to help the child to grow up. He can never do this if he remains a child himself. In this case the contact of maturity with immaturity, with its fructification of the latter, is missing, and the children are set back in their development. They are, then, in effect, children without parents. In certain American circles, so completely has the father become the playmate (and nothing more) of his child, that we have a whole generation of children growing up without fathers. Their begetter is there, but since he no longer *functions as a father*, these children are, psychologically speaking, half-orphans. They show, indeed, the characteristics of orphans. In England, too, it is not difficult to find circles where similar conditions prevail.

b. YOUTH UPROOTED

The whole problem is bound up with the insecurity of the present world-order. Large sections of youth, and those not the least intelligent, have become split off from the traditional roots of their being without having struck root elsewhere. As Keyserling says, the youthful *intelligentsia* of to-day seeks to obliterate the entire heritage of culture and morals which comes down from the past—the accumulated wisdom of the ages—and start again with a *tabula rasa*. This means, in practice, the return to a completely uncivilised state of society.

Very vivid glimpses of what this de-civilisation of humanity can amount to in practice are provided for us by Judge Lindsey, with his descriptions of the barbaric licence of very considerable circles of modern American youth—"petting-parties," where the girls have to be carried home, too drunk to walk, and where every conceivable liberty is taken with the girls (short, as a rule, of full sex intercourse); in short, where boys and their girl friends "let themselves go" to an extent which only a few years ago would have been impossible anywhere save in a brothel.

It will be said: "Oh, but we have nothing like this in England!" Are we so certain? It is true that the "petting-party" is not an institution on this side of the Atlantic. But those who imagine that the social upheavals brought about by the war, together with the economic emancipation of women, the loosening of parental control, the spreading far and wide of a knowledge of birth-control, and the revolution in habits resulting from motoring and week-ending, have left the moral life and habits of the English people untouched are living in a world of complete illusion.

All well-informed students of social matters are agreed that the last fifteen to twenty years have seen a very large increase in temporary sex unions of one sort and another.[1]

[1] In the *Woman's Journal* (August 1931) Mr. Clifford Bax writes: "Nobody . . . denies that sexual morality has vastly changed since 1900. . . . Thousands of young men and women now form temporary alliances in a more or less light-hearted spirit. The notion of 'sin' is to them as obsolete as the yet earlier notion of 'taboo.' . . . the lack of seriousness with which . . . [such alliances] are usually regarded has brought down the value of sexual experience to a perilously low point."

The change in our *mores* can be easily checked (in a rough way

It is (in my experience) the older generation alone which protests against such a statement as this (without in any way investigating the matter!). The young know well enough that moral conditions are so changed that their elders simply do not understand the world in which they live. This applies both to England and the United States.

A favourite remark with ostriches (when confronted with something they really *cannot* overlook) is: "Oh, but this is quite an *exceptional* case!" Yet as everyone with whom one discusses this question knows of similar cases, it does not appear, after all, that they are very exceptional! The truth is that people will go to almost any length in refusing to believe anything they do not want to believe. Ostriches may be divided into two classes: *bona-fide* ostriches, who are so much out of touch with modern life that they really believe the moral conditions in England are still the same as they were in Victorian

by staying in almost any week-end or pleasure resort in England and noticing the steady stream of young unmarried couples who arrive in cars or on motor-cycles to spend the night together.

On p. 43f. I have made it clear that I am not "attacking" or "libelling" either youth or any other section of the community. The present state of things is the almost inevitable result of a special set of circumstances. Formerly, as we all know, large numbers of girls were restrained from sex life though fear of maternity; now that this fear has been (to a large extent) removed, the consequence (human nature being what it is) is a great increase in extra-matrimonial relations. And when it is remembered that the other powerful factors mentioned above all work in the same direction, it is really noteworthy that these relationships are not much more numerous than they actually are. Just precisely how numerous they are cannot, of course, be estimated; there are considerable circles of English life still almost untouched by the new freedom—a fact which makes it difficult for those moving in them to realise how things have altered in other circles! In Scandinavia, as is well-known, the trial marriage is already a recognised institution, and in Austria the conditions are similar (although here Catholicism acts to some extent as a brake).

days; and pseudo-ostriches, who adopt the "How dare you libel our youth?" attitude, for the best of all possible reasons—self-defence!

As Judge Lindsey complains in his article "Wisdom for Parents" (see *Sex and Civilisation*, Allen & Unwin, p. 180), the parent or teacher of to-day is often completely blind to what is going on under his very nose. The Judge has been told by parents that he was grossly exaggerating the situation when, in some cases, he was actually helping (in secret) the children of these very parents to get out of sexual troubles. He has been bitterly attacked from the pulpit, for libelling "the clean youth of America," by a minister whose own daughter had come, without of course telling her parents, to take his advice as to the treatment of a venereal disease which she had contracted!

c. FREEDOM AND AUTHORITY

The existence of this great gulf between the generations is one of the deepest tragedies of our civilisation.

The parent is often impaled on the horns of a dilemma. If he remains true to his own inner life he runs the risk of losing touch altogether with his children, whose uprooted minds find no points of contact with his. If he meets them completely on their level and seeks too ardently to modernise and rejuvenate himself he may easily become insincere, and through tearing up his own roots cease to be capable of exerting any influence at all. In Germany, many of the older generation who interested themselves in the *Jugendbewegung* became so completely juvenile themselves that their presence was of no educational value

At this point, I know, some enthusiastic "modern" will exclaim: "Oh, but why *should* the older generation influence the younger? Why not leave the young people to work out their own problems?"

In a certain sense it is no doubt true that each generation must solve its own problems. But the point here in question is: Are the young people of to-day to work out everything for themselves (which means reversing the whole process of civilisation and going back to primordial innocence), or are they to learn something from the vastly greater experience of their elders, and from the store of knowledge and wisdom accumulated by centuries of culture? After all, no one would suggest that the boys and girls of to-day should refuse to accept the scientific knowledge handed down by previous workers, that every laboratory worker should himself personally estimate, at the cost of immense pains, the atomic weights of all the elements before he used a chemical equation!

The point of view of the "moderns" is, apparently, that while we have exact knowledge in (say) chemistry or mathematics, which can thus be passed on from one generation to another, there is no such thing as any body of transmissible knowledge in culture or morals. Some such opinion must lie behind the refusal to admit that in this field the older generation can teach anything to the younger.

This is one of those ideas which are so widely held in the world of to-day and yet never formulated. It is one of the concealed dogmas of those who have no dogmas.

It cannot, indeed, very well be formulated, because the moment it came out into the open its absurdity would become apparent. No one *really* believes that humanity in all the centuries of its evolution has learnt absolutely nothing, that the teaching of all the great seers and philosophers, not to mention the Churches, is entirely valueless. Yet this is the implication lying behind the argument that the young generation must work out its own salvation without any assistance from the older generation.

In reality it is clear that all civilisation depends upon a willingness to build, to a greater or less extent, upon the past. A sheer break with tradition means nothing less than pure barbarism. The attempt to act on the assumption that wisdom was born with us can only result in the collapse of all culture and morals. To-day this truth, however repugnant it may be to our South Sea islanders, cannot possibly be over-emphasised.

What the "modern" mind envisages is the total negation of everything that is not self-evident to a boy or girl in their 'teens. The whole of life is to be *cut down* to the level of adolescence. (In a recent ultra-modern publication—*Common-sense and the Child* (Ethel Mannin) —this aim is candidly admitted.)

. . . . .

To Keyserling we owe an extraordinarily interesting treatment of the parent-child problem (see *America Set Free*, pp. 266 ff.) in which he makes clear the intimate connection between this cult of immaturity (which is so characteristic of present-day western life) and the decline in the authority of the father, whose true rôle it is to represent, before the child, the realm of values and moral authority. For this purpose he must neither play the tyrant on the one hand (which will destroy his spiritual authority) nor attempt to be a mere comrade of his boy or girl.

"Wherever the fathers try to adapt themselves to their revolutionary sons, filial love is singularly rare," writes Keyserling (p. 293). The fact is that, subconsciously, the younger generation bears a grudge against the older for not having performed the educational task that was its duty. It must not be forgotten that the deeper desire of youth is for *growth*, and its craving for freedom, by comparison, a very superficial matter. It is not freedom which assists growth, but a wise combination of freedom and authority, and it is the failure of the modern father (and in many cases of the teacher) to provide the latter element that undermines their position in the eyes of youth. This is very strikingly illustrated by the fact that in modern movements, which have sprung from youth, the element of authority has been revived and given a foremost position. The enthusiasts for freedom are for the most part either women or elderly men with the mentality of the rebels of the Victorian age.

The problem of the adjustment of the two generations is the problem of human civilisation. If we are to save ourselves from a barbarous regression (called "emancipation") we must discover a method of bridging the fearful gulf described in this chapter. For this purpose a better understanding of youth is above all things necessary, and the next chapter will accordingly be devoted to a somewhat detailed examination of the psychology of youth.

Suggestions for reading in connection with Part I

KEYSERLING. *Creative Understanding. America Set Free.*
BABBITT, IRVING. *Democracy and Leadership.*
HAAS, DR. *What is European Civilisation?*
SPENGLER, OSWALD. *The Decline of the West.*
BENDA, JULIEN. *Belphegor.*
LIPPMANN. *A Preface to Morals.*
DAWSON, C. *Progress and Religion. Christianity and Sex.*
HUXLEY, ALDOUS. *Proper Studies.*
ARNOLD, MATTHEW. *Culture and Anarchy.*
EUCKEN, R. *Main Currents of Modern Thought.*
WALDO, FRANK. *The Re-discovery of America.*
RUSSELL, BERTRAND. *Principles of Social Reconstruction.*
MALINOWSKI. *The Sexual Life of Savages.*
MCDOUGALL, W. *World Chaos.*
INGE, DEAN. *Christian Ethics and Modern Problems.*
LEWIS, WYNDHAM. *The Doom of Youth.*
HUDSON, C. E. *Recent Psychology and the Christian Religion.*
INGRAM, K. *The Modern Attitude to the Sex Problem.*
BRIFFAULT, R. *Sin and Sex.*
KIDD, BENJAMIN. *Social Evolution.*
SMUTS, J. C. *Holism and Evolution.*

PART II

THE PSYCHOLOGY OF YOUTH

CHAPTER IV

THE NEW PSYCHOLOGY

a. INTRODUCTORY

The title of this section is perhaps hardly justifiable. There is to-day, properly speaking, no such thing as *the* psychology of youth.

It is inevitable that the present-day conflicts as to fundamentals should be reflected in psychology. The notion that it is possible to run away from all ultimate problems and construct a psychology of youth that shall be purely empirical is a great illusion. The manifest absurdities into which the behaviourist school has been led provide a sufficient commentary upon this statement. It is much better to face the present situation frankly and admit that we do not possess a definite psychology of youth, that the problems centring about the growth and development of the child and adolescent are matters of acute conflict.

A great deal of current literature on the psychology of childhood and adolescence represents a very unscientific hotchpotch of observed facts and views borrowed now from one school and now from another, as it suits the convenience of the writer. Worst of all, compilations of this sort are apt to be taken for gospel truth by the inexperienced reader, who swallows it all as "psychology."

Perhaps the most satisfactory method of approaching

the matter is to read the chief works of the various schools and then to form one's own conclusions. But how few of us can find the time to do this! And how few, again, are competent to judge between the rival points of view.

These introductory remarks are necessary in justice to the reader. As the situation stands it is not possible to present a clear outline of the psychology of youth. There are, in fact, as many psychologies of youth as there are *Lebensanschauungen*!

To the behaviourist, the growing child is moulded by its environment in a fashion which practically shuts out will and intelligence as real factors. (Mr. Aldous Huxley maintains that, to the behaviourist, it was a difference of environment alone which caused one boy to become Shakespeare and another the Stratford-on-Avon village idiot!)

To the eugenist, on the contrary, almost everything is heredity, and environment sinks far into the background.

To the convinced Freudian, the emotional and instinctive bents acquired in childhood are decisive, and the charge is often brought against him that he undervalues both heredity and later environmental and educational factors.

To the Adlerian, the purely individual tendencies, especially those associated with the will-to-power, are the most significant.

And so on.

In the following I propose to adhere, as far as possible, to well-established facts, and to indicate that any theories advanced are *theories* and not dogmas.

. . . . .

At present, it does not appear to the detached student that we possess more than a series of glimpses of the truth, seen from various angles.

The behaviourist, in stressing the significance of our reactions to outside influences, emphasises a factor formerly too much neglected; Freud, tracing personality back to infantile roots, makes a discovery which, within certain limits, is of immense value; Adler, in developing his psychology of self-assertion, does something towards overcoming the one-sidedness of Freud and his school; McDougall, analysing the instincts at the root of behaviour, provides a useful complement to the narrowness of the behaviourists. But the most misleading one-sidedness results when each school (as is so often the case) puts forward the claim to possess the whole truth. The antithesis Freud–Adler has to some extent been transcended by C. G. Jung (whose psychology combines many of the most valuable discoveries of the two and is widely regarded as the richest and deepest psychological system of to-day). In the future we may look to see this sort of synthetic work carried much farther. Very valuable beginnings in this direction have been made by W. Stern, Ed. Spranger, W. Hoffmann, and others. In the meantime, we can scarcely do more than endeavour to form a common-sense working psychology upon a basis which, from the point of view of the systematic thinker, is highly unsatisfactory.

b. A WORD OF CAUTION

The student of psychology must be on his guard against swallowing unprovable theories concealed as matter-of-fact statements. To take an example: Dr. Jung has warned us against the insidious "nothing but." In modern psychological works we find continually such statements as "idealistic love is nothing but a means employed by nature to propagate the species," or "poetry is nothing but sublimated sex." In such phrases lies concealed, to deceive the unwary, a naturalistic system of values not warranted by the facts. It may be true that the development of romantic love or the feeling for poetry in adolescence is connected with the biological urge of sex—no one, indeed, nowadays denies this. But the suggestion, implied in the above statements, that the animal instinct is the all-important thing, and the mental life connected with or accompanying it can be relegated to the "nothing but" category, is illegitimate. It is not scientifically demonstrable. We might, if we wished, reverse the process, and say "the sex instinct is nothing but the raw material from which nature makes poetry or romantic love." This statement is, strictly speaking, as good as the other!

In this and similar more or less subtle ways many present-day writers on psychology mask their naturalistic prejudices behind the suggestion that the material (whatever that may be) is in some unexplained way prior to the mental and emotional, and of superior reality and importance.

The opposite process, which consists in regarding as "real" or "true" only the mental or ideal and relegating the physical to a secondary position, is also dangerous, although, at the present time, less in evidence than the naturalistic tendency.

It is my plea that we should regard the facts of the psychology of youth objectively, and as far as possible free from imported valuations.

The all-important thing is the accomplished fact that human personality exists as a reality, with all its component parts—the physical body, the basic instincts, the higher mentality (the term "higher" is here used apart from valuation), and that these form a *whole*. That is the centre of the problem. The analysis of this whole with the object of demonstrating that a certain part is the "real" part, or the "basic" part, and the others more or less unreal or secondary, is, from the standpoint of a realistic examination, totally illegitimate. It is a species of philosophical (or anti-philosophical) propaganda, which can only introduce confusion into the investigation.

If, for example, we set out to examine childhood with the prior conviction that only the animal side of life is "real," we shall arrive at conclusions very different from those we should have arrived at had our method been unbiased.

. . . . .

To-day we incline, almost without knowing it, to think that because, from the standpoint of evolutionary naturalism,[1] the physical takes precedence in point of time, it should be regarded as in some way more "real" than the mental—which we regard, then, as secondary or derivative. If we allow ourselves to be carried away by this bias, our whole outlook may be vitiated at the outset.

[1] For a discussion of the exact meaning of the term "naturalism" the reader is referred to Dr. Rusk's book, *The Philosophical Bases of Education*, chap. iii. Herbert Spencer and T. P. Nunn may be taken as examples of educational naturalists. "Naturalism," says Rusk, "regarding all behaviour from the animal standpoint, takes instinctive activity as typical . . . it regards man's highest aspirations as illusions." Pushed to its logical conclusion, naturalism entirely disintegrates personality.

Time, in point of evolution, has nothing to do with the problems of psychology. The so-called "higher mentality" of man is an object of scientific study, precisely on a level with the instinctive and physical, however obscure the relationship between them may remain; and we must firmly resist what Mr. Tansley calls "the biological fallacy," the derivation of the "higher" from the "lower."[1]

It can scarcely be too much emphasised that psychology still suffers heavily from the attempt to impose upon it the methods of reductive analysis proper to (say) chemistry. The attempt to reduce personality, as we know it, to certain ultimate parts (whether called reflexes, instincts, thoughts, or ideas) and then to understand it through reintegration, as if it were sulphate of copper, may be regarded as having definitely failed.

"There is, within the framework of personality, nothing wholly isolated; under no circumstances does personality consist of elements (that is original components, the combination of which results in the person being formed). It is composed solely of factors which possess no self-dependent existence. The whole precedes the parts; and the whole is more real than the parts." (W. Stern, *Personalistische Psychologie*: from *Einführung in die neure Psychologie* (Saupe), p. 195.)[2]

[1] "Thought and emotion, as we know them, are absolutely *sui generis*, and we do not get the least nearer to an understanding of them by believing (or for that matter by disbelieving) that they are results of brain processes." (A. G. Tansley, *The New Psychology*, p. 26.) Chap. i of Charles Fox's *Educational Psychology* will be found helpful in giving a review of various theories of mind: on p. 14 he writes: "Any sound theory of the mind, since it is alive, must show analogies with living organisms."

[2] This statement does not commit us to support this or that school to the exclusion of others; because it is simply a statement of fact. Personality is a given reality in its form as a whole. It is when we

It is necessary to make these points clear because some readers may say: "You reject naturalism, and yet a large part of your argument draws upon instinct psychology!" No one denies the vast importance of instinct to-day. But at the same time it is possible to believe that personality contains other elements beside instinct. We need not straightway set up a system explaining *everything* on the instinctive basis! (For a definition of instinct, see *Social Psychology* (McDougall), chap. ii.)[1]

The school of psychology indicated in the quotation from Stern is now of rapidly increasing importance. It reverses the tendency (predominant until very recently) to explain psychic phenomena from the lower levels upwards; and, in dealing with the problems of youth and childhood, studies *actual* types and personalities rather than split-off portions (such as memory, will, feeling, reason, or any of the separate instincts), maintaining, indeed, that these elements in personality have no meaning at all save in relation to a complete personality. Stern, Spranger, Hoffmann, Klages (see *The Science of*

attempt the reduction of this whole to parts and say: it consists of instincts and these alone are real, or it is made up of reflex actions and these are the sole reality, or it is composed of soul and body and the soul is alone important, that we leave the ground of observed fact and embark upon speculation.

The behaviourist who says that reflex actions are scientific facts but instincts are imaginary abstractions is just as much a dogmatist as the theologian who says the soul is real and the study of reflex actions is a materialistic approach. Such dogmatism is, in McDougall's words, "a mark of scientific incompetence."

[1] In the Introduction to this work we are given a vivid picture of the absolute revolution by which the instincts have achieved their present dominant position in psychology. Such leading thinkers as H. Sidgwick and T. H. Green were ignorant, to an extent that seems to us almost incredible, of the true significance of instinct in the make-up of personality (although they may have been aware of ideal elements which are to-day too much thrust into the background).

Character), and others have done valuable work along these lines. The so-called *Gestalt* psychology is related to this tendency, and claims "that any cross-section of experience is a structural whole, the distinguishable features of which are not entities capable of independent existence, like the bricks of a wall—but rather are parts of a whole of which each part is organically related to all the rest." (McDougall: section entitled "Recent Developments of German Psychology" in *Social Psychology*; 21st ed., p. 247.)

c. FREUD, ADLER, AND JUNG

It would not be possible, within these limits, to give an adequate outline of the Freudian psychology (which is, of course, of immense importance for our topic).

It is assumed that the reader is acquainted at any rate with the more fundamental ideas of the psycho-analytical school, the deeper study of which is a life-task. One or two points only, of outstanding significance, can here be touched upon by way of introduction.

The mind as seen from the standpoint of the so-called New Psychology is no epiphenomenal affair or "integration of motor responses" (after behaviourist ideas); it is an active entity "endowed with psychic energy, just as the body is endowed with physical energy" (Tansley, p. 71), although we are still very much in the dark as to the relation between mental and physical energy. The mind is envisaged as an organism functioning according to its own laws and endowed with activity. This is a dynamic, as opposed to a mechanistic, psychology. The mind is active, and no mere arena of reflex actions.

As is well known, the concept of the *subconscious* plays

a very large part in the new psychology. Only a section of the mind—relatively small—comes into consciousness. The larger and by far the most significant and determinative part of the mind is below the level of our conscious life; like an iceberg, the mind shows above the surface but a fraction of its real content, and that fraction is often moved (at any rate very largely) from beneath. Down below (terms such as "above" and "below" are, of course, purely metaphorical and devoid of actual relation) lie layers of instincts, emotions, buried (though not forgotten) thoughts, memories of the past (both individual and racial), in fact, a veritable storehouse of the raw material of human life and action; and from time to time, according to the circumstances and the presence or otherwise of suitable stimuli, this material lies quiescent or springs to conscious life. We must not fall into the error of supposing that the below-the-water part of the mind (to retain the iceberg metaphor) is at any time purely passive, a mere dead-weight; it is a ballast without which the functioning of the conscious upper level would be unthinkable.[1]

The moment we ask more precise questions as to the content of this all-important subconscious region we are faced with the deep differences of opinion existing between the rival schools of thought. Freud, notoriously, lays a very heavy emphasis upon the sexual element, although, as he seems to understand by sexual almost the same thing as vital, his views are nearer to those of other thinkers than at first sight might seem to be the

[1] Dr. Glover—a leading exponent of Freudian psychology—speaks of the inherited instincts as "the raw material of the individual"; they remain throughout his life "the hidden sources of all his manifold activities." (Quoted by McDougall, *Social Psychology*, 21st ed., p. 426.)

case—in fact, it is open to doubt whether the Freudian idea of sex is very different from Bergson's *élan vital* or Schopenhauer's "will-to-live": McDougall seems to think they are practically the same thing.

Since Freudians explain child-life chiefly from the standpoint of the unconscious sex relationships of children and parents (boy-mother; girl-father), this school is described sometimes as "family psychology."[1] An enormous importance attaches, if we accept these viewpoints, to the ties of instinct during the first four or five years of life, which are determinative for the individual's future life to an extent formerly undreamed of; a nervous breakdown (say) at the age of sixty may have as true cause a shock received at the age of two or three! It is during these early years that the plastic subconscious absorbs impressions and takes on certain "sets" destined to mould it for life. (Thus, if a mother allows her baby to regard itself as the centre of the universe, the foundations may be laid of an ego-centric and ill-adapted character which may persist till old age; cf. p. 88).

Freud may thus be ranked amongst environmentalists,

[1] The following short extract from Freud's *Vorlesungen zur Einführung in der Psychoanalyse*, chap. xiii, gives the gist of his position. "Even as a little child, the boy begins to develop a peculiar tenderness towards his mother; he looks upon her as his *own*, and regards the father as his competitor, endangering his sole rights to the mother. In the same way, the small girl looks upon her mother as a person who imperils her tender relationship to her father, and takes up a position she could fill very well herself."

As is well known, the group of emotions centring around this mother-son relationship is called the Oedipus complex (after the Greek myth) and is one of the pillars of the psycho-analytical system (C. G. Jung, in particular, makes a great deal of the psychological value of ancient myths, which reflect, in his opinion, emotional and instinctive truths of immemorial antiquity, deeply embedded in the subconscious mind of the race).

if by environment we mean the immediate personal relationships of the child; but as an anti-environmentalist, if we take the term in the sense of mere external or intellectual influences (such as food—mental or physical, school influences, etc.) to which Freud attaches an extraordinarily low degree of significance as character-forming agencies. In fact, one of the main objections brought against this school (at any rate in its more extreme forms) is that it almost eliminates the intellect and will as formative influences, and makes of the child and young person the tool of instinctive forces of which they are often unconscious (although it is held, we must not forget, that curative treatment, along the lines of Freud, can, by delving down into the lower levels and resetting twisted portions, do a vast deal to remove the consequences of bad childhood influences). Upon the markedly anti-intellectual trend of the Freudian movement we have already commented (Chap. II); it has had enormous influence in the modern world, especially in literature and the drama.

Should we take Freud as our guide, it would follow that the proper development of a boy's or girl's instinctive life is beyond all comparison more significant than any intellectual or moral influences. Sex being looked upon as the basic motive force in life, the process of education becomes, to a large extent, a matter of helping the sex impulse to find its normal line of expression.[1] In the first place the emotional life of the infant centres in its mother, and later in life it is often a matter of great

[1] "Medical psychologists have for long been forced to see that the average child will develop on its intellectual side unchecked if the emotions and the instinctive dispositions are healthily finding their natural goals."—Dr. S. Read, *The Struggles of Male Adolescence*, p. 33 (*see also* the Introduction).

difficulty (contrary to what might be expected) to get this life redirected towards its normal racial goal—mating. The boy tends to refuse to grow up; in popular phrase, he wants to remain tied to his mother's apron-strings. Only the psycho-pathological specialist knows what a surprisingly large proportion of boys never pass through the intervening phases of self-centred sex interest and homo-sexually tinged eroticism to the true end-phase of an erotic fixation upon a life-partner, with fatherhood and the full assumption of racial responsibilities. (It is probable that a large amount of the celibacy amongst modern men is due far less to economic causes than to "premature fixation," or, in other words, the refusal of the erotic instinct to transfer itself to its normal object.) There are many grades of intermediate arrest. The boy may remain obstinately attached to his mother; he may stop at the ego-centric stage (the "selfish bachelor" type); or he may be arrested in a more or less homosexual stage, when his sex energy either fixes itself upon other men (as in the cases where we get actual unnatural vice) or turns into a more harmless (although anti-racial) preference for male society and lack of interest in the female. The civilised communities of to-day contain a large proportion of such types as these; and woe betide the girl who becomes attached to any one of them!

At the least, Freud has given us one of those bold epoch-making theories which, despite their over-simplification of the facts, compel a reorientation of thought, and thus lead on to a larger synthesis, when the first tide of advance (accompanied by exaggerations) is over and has yielded to a more mature valuation of the position.

It is by no means correct to look upon the Freudian

psychology as occupied wholly with the sexual side of the subconscious. Counterbalancing the sex instinct are the ego-impulses (*Ichtriebe*), which are concerned with the interests of the individual, and not with those of the race. In fact, the conflict which often occurs between these two basic tendencies in the subconscious is a source of mental and nervous illnesses (cf. *Vorlesungen*, chap. xxii).

The development of a psychology of the ego-centric impulses was the special achievement of Dr. Alfred Adler, whose system is based upon a somewhat one-sided stressing of the importance of the self-assertive elements in personality—the thwarting of these, rather than of the racial instincts, is, according to the school of Adler (individual psychology), the source of nervous troubles and defective development. The idea of the subconscious here falls very much into the background. This school, although an offshoot of the Freudian movement, has now reached a point at which there is little resemblance to the parent doctrine.

. . . . .

"Unfortunately, Adler goes so far that he almost entirely neglects the Freudian viewpoint, thus falling into a similar error of one-sidedness and exaggeration." Thus writes C. G. Jung (*Analytische Psychologie und Erziehung*, p. 34), whose psychology, as we have mentioned, is perhaps the most important, because the least one-sided and the most firmly grounded in experience and thought of all the different schools coming under the head of the New Psychology.

The soul-life of man, says Jung, is "a flow of activity

capable of kaleidoscope changes," according to the play of instincts: before his wedding-day a man's mind may be according to Freud, and afterwards according to Adler!

As Jung himself remarks, his point of view does not make things easy, "the eternally changing life of the soul is a greater truth, albeit a less comfortable one, than the cocksureness and rigidity of a one-sided viewpoint" (above, p. 34). With Jung we desert the deceptive over-simplification of the "nothing but" schools to take our stand upon the more solid ground of observation. We must not insist upon explaining everything before we know what it is (who knows what an instinct is?), but must stand upon the basis of psychological facts. "Our method is the comprehension of life" (p. 39).

To Jung "the unconscious is not merely secondary in origin, a storehouse of repressed complexes and unfulfilled desires, nor even of forgotten experience and racial tendencies, 'the sediment of all the experience of all time,' but also the source of inspirations and intuitions, and the home of our undeveloped potentialities—the submerged personality which is the complement of the mask that we show to the world." (J. H. Badley, *The Will to Live*, p. 246.)

We are indebted to Jung for a development of the concept of the unconscious that is one of the most remarkable and fruitful achievements of the New Psychology. (The study of Jung's great work, *The Psychology of the Unconscious*, will come as a veritable revelation to those who have previously read chiefly on the lines of the older schools.)

. . . . .

The time is still far distant when a truly scientific estimate of the permanent value of the New Psychology can be made. That it has opened up new fields of vast importance is incontestable. Freud has been called the Columbus of the mental life. But we are still too much in the dark as to the relationship between the new data and the biological and social aspects of psychology to be able to assign to the New Psychology its proper place in the study of psychology as a whole.

The following books are recommended (in addition to those already mentioned); those starred are perhaps the most suitable for beginners:

*James, William. *The Principles of Psychology* (still useful if read in conjunction with more recent works).

*McDougall, W. *An Outline of Psychology* (very useful). *Abnormal Psychology* (contains a valuable outline of psycho-analytical theories).

*Joad, C. E. M. *Mind and Matter.*

Fox, C. *The Mind and its Body.*

Koffka. *The Growth of the Mind.*

Young, K. *Social Psychology.*

*Ogden, C. K. *The A.B.C. of Psychology.*

Woodworth, R. S. *Psychology* (the most widely read American work).

*Adams, Sir John. *Everyman's Psychology.*

*Aveling, F. "Psychology" (in *An Outline of Modern Knowledge*. Ed. Rose). *Personality and Will.*

Jung, C. G. *Contributions to Analytical Psychology. Psychological Types.*

*Corrie, J. *A.B.C. of Jung's Psychology* (short and simple)

Coriat. *What is Psycho-Analysis?*

*JONES, ERNEST. *Psycho-Analysis* (Benn's Sixpenny Library).

FREUD, S. *Introductory Lectures on Psycho-Analysis. The Psycho-Pathology of Everyday Life.*

LOW, B. *The Unconscious in Action.*

FLÜGEL, J. C. "Theories of Psycho-Analysis" (in *An Outline of Modern Knowledge.* Ed. Rose).

WATSON, J. B. *Psychology from the Standpoint of a Behaviourist.*

*KING, W. P. (ed.). *Behaviourism*—a symposium (anti-behaviouristic).

WATSON and MCDOUGALL. *The Battle of Behaviourism* (a debate).

HOGBEN, L. *The Nature of Living Mind.*

KÖHLER. *Gestalt Psychology.*

ROBACK, A. *The Psychology of Character.*

BURT, C. *The Young Delinquent.*

CHAPTER V

CHILDHOOD

a. A SKETCH OF DEVELOPMENT
b. THE CHILD

a. A SKETCH OF DEVELOPMENT

It is convenient to divide human life into five stages—infancy, childhood, youth, maturity, and old age.

A generation ago it would have been supposed that a study of sex in relation to education would have been concerned almost entirely with the third stage. But we now know that sex life has its very significant beginnings in infancy and childhood. In fact, the five stages can hardly be regarded separately. They form a process each phase of which requires for its understanding some reference to the other phases.

A great deal of difference of opinion exists as to the best definition of these stages. Generally speaking, the period from birth to the sixth or seventh year is regarded as infancy or early childhood; the period from seven to eleven or twelve is pre-puberty (a "marking-time" stage, when growth is less rapid and the child attains to a certain stability preceding the revolution of puberty); and the years between about twelve until twenty-one (nineteen for girls) form the adolescent stage. The term "adolescence" is, however, used by some writers to denote the post-puberty stage from about seventeen onwards until maturity.[1]

[1] The Romans understood by *adolescentia* the period between *puer*

There is not, of course, anything hard and fast about these divisions. In Italy or Spain the crisis of puberty may take place as much as two or three years earlier than in England. Amongst Jews, too, even when resident in northern lands, sex development is more rapid. The reference here is to normal cases in our own race.

Contrary to what is often supposed, the mental and physical aspects of puberty are not parallel. This fact speaks strongly against the view that the mental side of personality is a mere reflex or upper level of the physical—the ultra-materialistic view widely held until recent years. According to this theory the ripening of the bodily powers should bring with it as a corollary the appropriate mental and emotional symptoms. "It is necessary to differentiate strictly between the durations of psychic and physical puberty" (Bühler, p. 20).

It is, says Bühler, precisely the great prolongation of the mental side of puberty which makes the problem of adolescence in modern life so difficult—the higher the form of life the longer it takes for inward ripeness to be accomplished; the soul, in accordance with its greater complexity, has more to do to complete its adjustment with life. The reader is hence cautioned against regarding the process of becoming mature mentally as dependent directly upon the physiological side of the problem. We know as yet practically nothing of the real relationship between the bodily changes of puberty and the psychic developments. In speaking of maturity, it will

and *juvenis*, from about 15 to as much as 30 years. (C. Bühler, *Das Seelenleben des Jugendlichen*, p. 21.)

Dr. Spranger (the leading present-day German authority on adolescence) finds that for the North German city population adolescence should be regarded as the period from 13 to 19 for girls, and 14 to 22 for boys. (*Psychologie des Jugendalters*.)

thus be seen that everything depends upon whether we mean physical or psychic maturity.

Much depends, too, upon sex. That girls are older in every way than boys of the same nominal age is, of course, well known, although the true extent of the difference is not often realised. (Dr. K. Young, for example, in his *Social Psychology* (p. 179), makes the interesting observation that the age of girls, as measured by bone structure, is at thirteen years no less than two and a half years in advance of that of boys, and even at the age of four is a full year ahead.) A girl of eighteen is really about the same age as a boy of twenty-one, a fact of considerable significance both for education and practical life: if a man wishes to marry a wife of the same *real* age as himself she must be three or four years younger in years.

. . . . .

The precise nature of the mental and emotional changes which take place at puberty is not easy to define. Growth does not take place in a straight line. The boy does not grow gradually more and more manly. Normally, the boy of eleven is more self-confident than the lad of sixteen. The influx of new feelings and the need for difficult adjustments tend to disturb the psychic life of the boy or girl and to give rise to a period of insecurity, which only much later gives way to a new and stronger confidence.

What is the real *meaning* of this critical period?

Broadly speaking, the boy of eleven or twelve years has not yet discovered either himself or the world. He lives, to a very large extent, in the imaginary world of childhood. He *cannot*, indeed, know himself as yet, for the good reason that a large part of himself is not yet in existence; nor does he possess the mental capacities needful for an understanding of real life. Such understanding as he *seems* to have is imitative and unreal.

Spranger states that the decisive elements in the "new psychic organisation" are the discovery of the ego; the gradual formation of a life-plan; and the establishment of contact with the adult world (p. 38 of the work mentioned on p. 93).

From the standpoint of the New Psychology the period of early infancy (birth to the fourth or fifth year) and the adolescent period are the two most critical life-stages. In infancy the life-impulse receives its original "set" in the narrow surroundings of the family, while, in adolescence, the impulse, now deeper and stronger, takes up its attitude towards its own higher self and towards sex and life in the larger sense.

"There is a great expansion of the consciousness of self, with a desire to excel others . . . individual opinions begin to be held, ideals of various sorts have their birth . . . a certain amount of excessive egoism is likely . . . the character and personality become more or less set." Self-criticism, morbid sensitiveness, hero-worship, sexual interests accompanied often by acute embarrassment, and ethical conflicts are all characteristics of the stage. Thus writes Dr. Stanford Read (*The Struggles of Male Adolescence*, pp. 44–5). An outgrowing of the dream world of childhood and adjustment to the real world is the keynote of this critical phase, and many of its difficult problems arise either from a reluctance to leave childhood behind, or from a too eager desire to become adult.[1]

[1] Over-absorption in sport and games—which, unless regarded as purely recreative, belong, more or less, to the child phase—is a

We may regard this search for reality, this flight from the nest to discover the world, from different points of view. We may agree with the Bühler school and look upon it chiefly as the craving of the *ego* to enlarge itself through finding the "other" (both in the form of the outer world and in the narrower sense of the human partner);[1] or we may take up the more metaphysical viewpoint that the whole process can be brought under the head of *self-realisation*.

The trend of the life-impulse is always towards expansion, completion; like an organism it grows and sends out shoots, seeking always to attain its maximum development.[2] The quest for the "other," the search for reality, is only another name for self-completion, because the *ego* cannot fulfil itself in isolation and therefore seeks for contact with outer reality as a necessity of its own realisation.

It is therefore quite possible to regard the process of adolescence as the critical stage in the *becoming whole* of the human organism. If understood in the right sense, this affords an explanation of all the phenomena of the psychology of youth.

b. THE CHILD

The more we incline to the Freudian outlook the more importance must we attribute to the first four or five

symptom of the former tendency, and a precocious interest in girls, smoking, reading unsuitable literature, etc., of the latter.

The popular notion that the football-playing type of boy is "manly," while the student type is effeminate, is totally wrong (save perhaps in a physical sense)—it is the latter who is seeking to become an adult through knowledge, while the former is often trying to remain a child because he is afraid of adult problems and responsibilities.

[1] Dr. C. Bühler, *Das Seelenleben des Jugendlichen.*

[2] A very clear exposition of this conception is to be found in the first part of Dr. Hadfield's well-known work *Psychology and Morals.*

years of life. To quote two leading exponents of the New Psychology: "the foundations of our own mental life (apart from that which has been inborn) are laid down in the first five years of life," says Dr. Stanford Read; and Dr. Hadfield states that, in the opinion of most psycho-therapeutists, "all functional nervous disorders, even of later life, such as the breakdown of the girl of eighteen, the woman of thirty, or the business or professional man of fifty-five, originate in childhood."

Writers of the heredity school will be unwilling to assign so much importance to early environmental factors (and it is possible that such statements as the above demand a good deal of qualification); but in spite of such differences of outlook there is general agreement that these early years are of immense importance. Even if we believe that heredity is responsible for the larger part of our make-up, it is still true, as proved by experience, that inherited factors may be decisively modified by early influences. All parents should therefore realise the vital character of this first stage of development. There is a vast deal of truth in the old saying that the first step in the education of children is the education of their parents!

We must grasp the fact that the psychology of the child is quite other than that of the adult. Entire areas of personality which play a large part in the life of the grown-up are absent in the child; and there is a world of fancy peculiar to children into which the adult can hardly penetrate. While the recapitulation theories of the Herbart–Ziller school, and the genetic psychology of Stanley Hall, are now largely discredited, they contain a certain element of truth; the child does pass through mental stages, corresponding roughly to those of the savage. He is still unaware of reality, as the civilised man understands it, that is of the ordered universe created by logic and science, and dwells for much of his time in a world where dolls talk, animals are his friends and equals, and where the line of demarcation between the ego and the environment (the beginning of civilisation) is barely recognised. (Cf. Piaget, *The Child's Conception of the World*.) Of the real, inner workings of the child-mind we still know surprisingly little, in spite of the large output of work on child psychology.

. . . . .

The vexed question of the sexuality or otherwise of the child is largely a matter of *terminology*. The young child is not consciously sexual in feeling, but there is now a large amount of evidence revealing a subconscious sex life even in very young children.

In addition to the special nature of the family attachments (mother and son, father and daughter) which, as we have seen, is of so much significance in the New Psychology, we note in most cases the appearance in quite young children (even under one year) of sex differences of a psychological kind. The boy-baby is usually more decisive in his movements and more active and aggressive than his little sister. These and similar differences become specially marked when games are begun. The preference of little boys for soldiers and engines rather than dolls is incontestable. It has been argued (for example, by Mrs. C. P. Gilman) that boys prefer these things because they are told they ought to play with them, that the difference is due rather to suggestion than to a true psychological difference; but there is no evidence in favour of this theory. Moreover, boys usually prefer to do the things they are told not to do, and I feel convinced that if a small boy were told he "ought" to use the same toys as his sister that would only increase his enthusiasm for engines and instruments of destruction!

From our standpoint, especially, the most significant characteristic of early childhood is that the mind has not yet become canalised. Hence the frantic repetition which is so typical of the young child; it is seeking to make channels in the mind through repeating again and again the same action or sound. Professor Preyer found that a fourteen months old baby which persisted in opening and shutting the lid of a tin repeated the action, when allowed to continue, seventy-nine times! (Quoted by Hoffmann, *Die Reifezeit*, p. 31.) The small child may be envisaged (speaking psychologically) as a mass of unformed instinct-life, enormously sensitive to impressions, and absorbent to an almost incredible extent, yet containing within itself definite lines of development laid down by its inborn constitution. Just as the acorn *must* become an oak, and can never become a sycamore, the baby of a given race and type *must* develop along the lines of that race and type (subject, of course, to a certain degree of environmental modification). A Chinese baby does not become English when reared in England; and twins will show astounding resemblances, even when very differently brought up.[1]

[1] Behaviourism overlooks to an extent that is astonishing the obvious influence of the inborn factors; according to the doctrines of this school—supposing them to be applied to the vegetable world—it would be possible to grow sycamore trees from acorns, if one used the right sort of soil and manure. Nothing can ever alter the fact that

Modern psychology indicates that the libido[1] of the child (and very often even of the boy or girl in the adolescent years) is not fixed: it has not yet found a definite channel along which to flow. The inward insecurity which so frequently accompanies the critical teens, and is sometimes a cause of acute distress both to the young person and his or her parents, is understandable from this standpoint. The mainstream of the unconscious has not yet decided exactly in what direction to pour out its energy.[2] Normally, of course, the libido (after going through intermediate stages, see p. 111) should attach itself to its biological function, mating and parenthood. Any other course, although not of necessity injurious to the subject, is *abnormal* from a strictly biological viewpoint. Sublimation may be possible for certain types; but if everybody were to sublimate their

the dominating factor in the development of a living organism is that mysterious something which it brings into the world as *the form-giving principle*: ". . . the present endeavour of some biologists and psychologists to abolish the mystery of heredity by denying it all but a very slight influence on human and animal behaviour, seems to me ridiculous." (McDougall, *Social Psychology*, p. 417, 21st ed.)

[1] The much-discussed term *libido* is here used in the original and stricter sense of the emotional and instinctive energy associated with the sex life, and not (as with some writers) in the vaguer sense of psychic energy in general. We cannot here pursue the question of how far it is practicable to distinguish between one kind of psychic energy and another—it is certainly possible that, in the last analysis, all the types of energies are the same. But this is of academic interest at present. In the *Vorlesungen zur Einführung in die Psychoanalyse* (chap. xxvi) Freud writes: "We reserve, with justice, the term *libido* for the instinctive forces of the sexual life," and adds that he does not perceive any advantage in widening the term to include all or any instinctive energies, and coining a new term for the specifically sexual.

[2] In the *Vorlesungen zur Einführung in die Psychoanalyse* (chap. xxii) Freud gives a description of the fluidity of the libido, which enables it to flow now along one psychic channel, now down another.

sexual energy the world would come to a speedy end. It is therefore impossible to regard any development of boyhood or girlhood other than ultimate parenthood as being, properly speaking, *normal*. Even a marriage of sterility, by means of birth-control, is not normal, and from the standpoint of modern psychology may be highly injurious, since it represents frustration of the libido.

It may be objected that this is not the place in which to take up this matter, that it belongs more properly to the section dealing with adolescence. On the contrary, it is precisely at this stage that we should take hold of the idea that the future of the boy or girl depends to an immense extent upon the channel struck out by the libido in these early years—"during this period [the first year or two of life] the reflex bases of the sex instinct and the rudiments of the emotion accompanying the instinct are laid down as a result of the infant's relation to its mother. This is one of the most important practical discoveries of Freud." (A. G. Tansley, *The New Psychology*, p. 95.)

We may conceive of sex instinct in the child as being "diffused and primitive" (Tansley). It is a vague feeling, slumbering in the unconscious, capable of developing normally and also capable of being thwarted, hindered, or perverted. (The development of sexual perversity is only very rarely associated with physical peculiarities. A too tender mother may stimulate the latent libido and in this way cause grave trouble to be laid up for her offspring. Or she may be too severe and repressive, when the libido may be inhibited and driven underground, to come up later in the form of neurosis.

It is, I think, of great importance to realise that the normal track of the libido expression is not laid down from birth by nature in any final way (as might well be supposed); just because the human soul is so much more highly organised (even in the baby) than the animal soul, so its possibilities of becoming *détraquée* are infinitely greater. The direction of the libido along the true channel is a main task of the parents and educators of the child. In the past, although the psychology of the situation was not understood, methods of education were worked out which often, in a rough, practical way, accomplished very well what we now seek to do in a more scientific way—frequently with less success, in consequence of the bewildering variety of educational theories now before the public!

At this point we see with peculiar clearness how absolutely vital to the work of education is the impact of a form-giving influence upon the plastic mentality of youth. Failing such, we tend to get arrested development, the mind of the boy or girl remaining in an unorganised and infantile state. Entirely erroneous is the idea (to-day so popular in certain circles) that the absence of such an influence produces originality and personality (cf. pp. 107 and 113).

The child-mind may be regarded as a bundle of loosely related groups of instincts (although this is not the whole of the truth), and it is possible at a very early age to determine to some extent which of these instincts shall be developed and which checked. It is from this point of view that we can best consider the question of the training of the young child. The two chief instinctive tendencies are the sexual (in the widest sense) and the self-assertive.

Dr. Stanford Read (*The Struggles of Male Adolescence*, p. 28), speaking of the baby, says "the instinct of self is used to dominate his surrounding," and he goes on to explain, in a chapter which may be read by all parents with profit, how the doting parent who rushes to answer her babe's slightest cry, can, while meaning so well, lay the foundations of a character which believes the world must give him everything for which he cries loud enough. It is most important that this craving for power, which (after the nutrition impulse) is the earliest manifestation of child mentality, should not be allowed to become established (in the case of weakly children the danger is doubled). If this psychic channel be cut in early months and years a large part of the libido may flow into it and much of the energy which might have taken on a racially useful course will be deflected.

The opposite mistake, that of keeping the child under a too repressive discipline—although nowadays much less often perpetrated—is also to be taken very seriously. This may give rise to a timid and dependent type of character, or it may provoke a violent compensatory reaction—we all know of boys reared in strict homes who kicked over the traces the moment they tasted freedom!

Those who are responsible for the rearing of the child should, even in these earliest years, steer their course with some reference to the rocks ahead. The dangers most usually to be expected are the fixation of the libido upon the mother, after the time when it should take a wider course; the turning inwards of the libido (self-fixation); the arrest of the libido at the intermediate stage of friendship (a phase which, in more serious cases, may turn into dangerous homo-sexuality); and the weakening of the libido, through lack of nourishment (resulting in low vitality and lack of interest in life, especially in the opposite sex). It must not, of course, be supposed that these possibilities are sharply defined or mutually exclusive. For example, the mother-complex is very often found in conjunction with the last-named trouble.

The contemplation of these dangers should not, however, make the parent or teacher unduly anxious (that is the worst possible state of mind), for the reserve of vitality implanted by nature in the young is fortunately large enough, normally, to carry the boy or girl safely through these perils of youth—even when alarming collisions with rocks cannot be avoided!

Can any useful practical conclusions for this stage of education be drawn from the above considerations? To answer as briefly as possible: Attend to the physical health of the child—do not force mental development. Do not allow the child to dominate. If the question be asked: how is this to be prevented without repressing budding impulses? the reply is that a discipline should be established which is loving *yet* firm, and is not felt by the child as a tyranny because it is impersonal and accurately adapted to his needs. It is a great error to suppose that children like unlimited freedom.[1] On the

[1] Nothing could be more misleading than the notion that children cannot be happy unless they are always "having a good time." This is an entirely superficial deduction from the "no repressions" school of psychology; the soul of the child has various layers and currents, and deep down in the mind slumbers the spirit which demands adventure, difficulties to be overcome, risks, and disciplines. It is more dangerous to repress this element in mentality than to repress the craving for amusement. The skilful educator has a wide opportunity in helping the child to decide *which tendencies in his make-up are to develop and which are to be held back*. The make-everything-easy school allows the surface tendencies free play while checking (by starvation) the development of the deeper and more heroic elements in personality. The child actually *suffers* when thus allowed

contrary, they prefer true discipline. The right freedom is that which allows the child free play for its normal outlets (activity, play, helpfulness, etc.), but never allows it to impose its self-will tyrannically upon others. Fathers should not be afraid that if they come to represent, in the child-mind, the principle of authority, they will for this reason become unpopular. This is precisely what the child, subconsciously, demands from the father, who may thus, at the very outset of life, do something to introduce the young life to the objective world-order to which it must later learn adaptation.[1]

Children should be treated as children, and not be overmuch in the society of adults—especially if the adults are mentally active!

Atmosphere is immensely important: unhappiness, tension, anxiety, fear, conflict, or, on the other hand, "sloppy" sentimentality in the home are thoroughly bad. Children are enormously absorbent. A simple cheerful home-life (preferably in a family of several children) in which the children are not too much in the limelight is without doubt the ideal environment from a psychological standpoint.[2]

to degenerate; hence the unhappiness and restlessness of so many modern children, in the midst of an environment which, to outward seeming, does everything to help them.

[1] Cf. Keyserling, *America Set Free* (pp. 266 ff.), where there is a very penetrating treatment of the father-function in education.

[2] A vast mass of facts relating to child psychology has been accumulated by workers such as Preyer, Stanley Hall, Sully, Baldwin, Tracy, and Meumann, but the theoretical side of the subject is exceedingly indefinite. W. Stern's *The Psychology of Early Childhood* is perhaps the most significant modern work; while Koffka's *The Growth of the Mind* is also valuable.

The following works, amongst many others, will be found valuable for further reading in connection with Chapters V and VI:

OGDEN, R. M. *Psychology and Education.*

FOX, C. *The Mind and its Body.*

KOFFKA. *The Growth of the Mind.*

HALL, STANLEY. *Adolescence* (still of great value).

FIRTH, V. M. *The Machinery of the Mind.*

CHADWICK, M. *Difficulties in Child Development.*

MEREDITH, C. *The Bearings of Modern Psychology on Educational Theory and Practice.*

CRICHTON-MILLER. *The New Psychology and the Teacher.*

BLANCHARD, P. *The Child and Society. The Adolescent Girl.*

ADLER, A. *The Education of Children. Guiding the Child.*

WEXBERG, E. *Individual Psychology and Sex.*

FREUD, ANNA. *Introduction to Psycho-analysis for Teachers.*

SLAUGHTER, J. *The Adolescent.*

KIMMINS, DR. C. W. *The Mental and Physical Welfare of the Child.*

CHAPTER VI

ADOLESCENCE

a. ADOLESCENCE AND THE NEW PSYCHOLOGY

While the profound significance of the New Psychology in relation to early childhood is now almost universally recognised, the situation is less clear when we come to consider the period of puberty and adolescence.

It is very much open to doubt how far the relationships which now begin to form between the instinct life of the boy or girl and the world of moral and intellectual values can be adequately explained from this standpoint alone—although the side-lights thrown from thence are of great value.

It is certain that the attempt to explain the developments of adolescence from a purely instinctive standpoint is likely to lead us into a position that is too one-sided. Some of the foremost present-day German psychologists have recently drawn attention to the very serious difficulties which confront us when we seek to interpret adolescence as a mere unrolling of instinctive life. This is bound to result in a neglect of the psychic forces associated with *geistiges Leben*—the world of mind in the narrower sense.

How, for example, are we to explain the immense enthusiasm with which a clever boy will throw himself into the study of (say) chemistry? Even the most extreme Freudian could hardly expect us to believe that a love of chemistry is "nothing but" a sublimation of sex! Again, the romantic and quite ultra-physical erotic feeling which often invades the soul of boy or girl in the teens is not easily understandable on purely instinctive lines. Sex attraction on the physical plane can, of course, be thus explained. But the idealistic attitude towards sex of—to take an example—the best type of English boy of seventeen is another matter. Ultimately this attitude is without doubt related to the primary sex instinct. But this does not *explain* it. It is all very well to say that the racial instinct takes this very roundabout way of reaching its ends. These are mere words. *Why does it take this way and not the direct way of immediate sex attraction?* That is the problem! If we were able to answer this profoundly important question we should understand vastly more about the psychology of adolescence than is now possible. What is the mysterious power which lifts the human sex instinct up to the level of dream and vision, poetry and pure yearning? Such considerations are pointers turning our gaze in the direction of a world of *mind* which cannot in any simple way be related to or derived from the world of the unconscious, and indicating that points of view other than those of the New Psychology are needful if we are to *understand* (and not merely explain in words) the life of the adolescent. (For a lengthy treatment of this and related problems the reader is referred to Ed. Spranger's standard work, *Die Psychologie des Jugendalters* (Quelle und Meyer), especially chap. v.)

The endeavour on the part of many exponents of the New Psychology to treat the whole sphere of moral values and ideal concepts as something illusory is, in popular phrase, "not good enough." As Spranger very pertinently points out, this view leads to conclusions which are untenable. If the moral sense of man is something so utterly secondary as we are asked to believe it is, how does it come about that instinct itself is so often frustrated by a sense that is supposed to be "nothing but" a pale reflection of the true vital forces? How does it come about that the derivative is often stronger than the basic? To take an example. Suppose a monk dams up his sex life, and diverts it into the channel of doing good work amongst the poor. The Freudian would say that his libido, being frustrated, has found a new channel and cut its way along this. Subjectively, this may be the truth, but there is here no explanation of how it can occur that an abstract passion, like the monk's, can ever become so strong that it is able to dam up what the Freudian regards as something far stronger than any abstract passion. It is as if a river dammed itself. What is this "other than sex" which can become stronger than sex? The theory of the *Ichtriebe* (see p. 73) breaks down here. While it is obvious that human life requires, as a condition of its development (this is especially important in relation to the psychology of adolescence), a principle supplementing or counterbalancing sex capable of checking the instinct and sublimating a portion of it (otherwise we should have no morality, art, or literature!), the New Psychology does not account for this non-sexual principle in any adequate way. Sometimes, it is true, there is a Freudian conflict between sex and ego, but there is a whole world of objective mental life (including the exact sciences) which cannot be brought under the head of ego. The whole problem of the tensions existing between the instinct life and the so-called higher mental life is wrapped in obscurity.

The facts that the psycho-analytical school have collected are of incalculable significance, but we do not yet possess the true perspective from which to interpret them; and only too often the new material is linked up with a superficial and obsolete type of materialism which seeks always to explain the "higher" from the "lower."

It is all very well to say, with Freud, that the expression of instinct has been inhibited by social conventions; but if the whole of human life arises from the workings of instinct, how is it that these conventions, running contrary to our strongest instincts, have come into being at all? The influence of religion, say the "moderns." But this only pushes the problem back another stage! Why do people believe in religions which go against their instincts, if life consists solely of instinct? This is inexplicable from the naturalistic standpoint.

b. THE FLIGHT FROM THE NEST

The profoundly significant period of adolescence lies in between two periods of relative stability, late childhood and early maturity. The boy of twelve is complete as a child, and the young man in the early twenties is (in basic essentials) complete as a man, further development taking place, normally, along lines laid down during the critical years.

The boy of twelve or thirteen is normally in a state of stable equilibrium, happily adapted to his childish environment. Then comes adolescence, "with such profound new upheavals that one may, with justice, speak of a second birth" (Spranger). It is an individual matter whether the revolution takes place slowly or with a rush. But under all circumstances "the process comes from within, out of the growth of the soul itself" (Spranger). Some influence—retarding or accelerating—may, of course, be exerted by external factors, but a crisis there must be in all normal cases.

Speaking broadly, the higher the type the more serious the disturbances are likely to be. An entirely new synthesis of personality has to be effected, and the richer and more varied the mental and instinctive make-up of the boy or girl, the more difficulty will there be in achieving the approximate harmony which marks successful maturity. Parents should not be over-alarmed at the sufferings and struggles, or "naughtinesses," which may be part of this difficult period. In the lives of notable men how often do we not read of their troubles during these years! On the other hand, a smooth and easy passage through this period of transition is frequently indicative of a superficial nature, and of a lack of sexual vigour.[1]

. . . . .

[1] The following admirable summary is from Maher's *Psychology* (p. 152): "The period of *youth*, covering the next seven years [i.e. from fourteen onwards] marks the final 'setting' of the character in various directions. Whilst the memory and imagination continue active, the intellectual faculty of abstract conception, judgment, and reasoning rapidly expands, and the power of introspection also increases. The emotions and passions come into prominence. This is especially the season for building up *ideals*. It is the age of enthusiasm, of poetry, and of fancy, but it is also the epoch during which our most important intellectual convictions and moral habits crystallise and determine for good or ill the course of our whole future life." It might be added that deep-going alterations in convictions and moral habits after this period is over usually indicate either instability or exceptional spiritual force.

Behaviourism even less than the New Psychology can explain the fateful years of adolescence. However much the environment may modify development, it is of quite secondary importance at this time as compared with the fundamental biological changes.

"Puberty is first and foremost a biological fact, linked up with the rhythm of development which so clearly divides the life of man, from the earliest years to old age, into definite phases . . . regarded from the biological standpoint, puberty is the time when the young human seeks to fly away from the nest." Thus writes Walter Hoffmann, a leading German psychologist of the "structure psychology" school (*Die Reifezeit*, p. 67).[1]

The restlessness, the thirst for new experiences, the formation of all sorts of fantastic plans, and many other typical symptoms of earlier adolescence can all be viewed from this standpoint.

Hoffmann warns us especially, however, against interpreting adolescence *exclusively* from the biological side, and regarding the mental and emotional changes as mere consequences of the physical. Whatever the relationship may be, it is not so simple as this. In fact, many of the most characteristic phenomena of youth speak against such immediate connection between the mental and physical. For example, extreme shyness in the presence of the opposite sex is a very common symptom of puberty, although if the emotional changes depended directly upon the biological, we should expect physical sex attraction to follow more or less directly upon the

[1] In *Sex*, by Professors Patrick Geddes and J. A. Thomson, we find a clear, short account of the physical aspects of the period—the "bodily ripening," the changes in glandular functioning, bone structure, the sexual organs, metabolism, and so forth. Stanley Hall's *Adolescence* contains a much more detailed account.

maturing of the organs of sex. Also it is not unusual for a boy with a quite normal physical sex development to be (for a period) markedly homo-sexual in his emotional life (not to mention the not uncommon cases of permanent homo-sexuality in which the organs are perfectly normal). The old-fashioned idea that the mental in this age is, as it were, an outgrowth of the physical, requires, therefore, considerable modification. The whole problem is one of immense complexity.

If puberty were a simple matter of the child becoming sexually mature, and then going out into the world to find a mate—as it is with animals (in the main)—all would be plain sailing. The actual situation is far otherwise.

The complex organisation of the human mind, in its conscious and unconscious aspects, is the cause of the great variety of conflicts and difficulties of all sorts which arise at this stage. The over-simplification of the problems of adolescence under behaviourist influences is most deceptive.[1] A boy may develop organically in the healthiest way, but his mind may be so fixed on home attachments that he entirely fails to cut out the channels establishing contact with a wider reality, so that even at the age of (say) twenty-five he may still be a child. Another may be powerfully attracted to the opposite sex, but his ego impulses may be too strong to allow his

[1] Thus regarded, nothing could be more foolish than the notion (occasionally to be met with in ultra-modern sex literature) that the smooth and easy way in which the boys and girls of certain simple races pass through their adolescence is a model for us to copy; in reality it is just because they are not civilised and their mental life is on a low level of organisation and differentiation that such peoples are able to avoid many of the troubles that are the price of a higher culture. If we were all turnips we could very easily solve our sexual and social troubles! The attempt to do away with the difficulties of civilisation by refusing to be civilised is pure retrogression.

sex life any scope; he may devote himself to "getting on" with such energy that his emotional and instinctive life stagnates, giving rise to an arrest of another type. Again, the influence of some special social tendency may bring about surprising deflections from the normal line of development—as, for example, the wholesale flight of young men and women to a monastic life which took place during the later Middle Ages; or the cult of excessive athleticism in many modern girls' schools, which very frequently leads to otherwise normal girls becoming unfitted for sex life or maternity.

Most of these manifestations can be classified under the head of *failure to cross the gap which separates childhood from maturity*. The reconstruction of soul-structure, which is the essence of "growing up," for some reason fails to take place. A girl who is "crazy" about sport at the age of twenty has grown up physically, but her mental energy is still attached to the centres which fixed it in later childhood; the normal transference of energy to a fertilisation of the emotional and erotic fields has not been accomplished. The fear of adult life is often at the bottom of these states. It is *easier* to play tennis than it is to take up the responsibilities of a woman's life—husband, children, tiresome servants, rates and taxes![1]

. . . . .

The function of the educator during the period of early adolescence is fairly clear. His work is to help his pupil to cross the gap; to encourage him to develop and control, stage by stage, his newly-awakening powers and to

[1] "The general key to all these cases of abnormal behaviour of the libido is to be found in the tendency of energy to be expended along the line of least resistance" (Tansley, p. 111).

relate them effectively to the approaching tasks of adult life. Parents must understand that the flight from the nest is a perfectly natural and wholesome phase; above all, they must not seek to tie their offspring down or clip their wings. A reaction against childish things, taking the form, with some types, of rebelliousness, truculence, unpleasant self-assertion, and so on, should be sympathetically dealt with and never treated as "badness." Even extreme manifestations of this sort may mean very little; they are the first crude symptoms of a new egoistic force which should later develop into strength and purpose. The secret is to lead the new forces into educationally useful paths. A boy who makes himself almost impossible at home at the age of fourteen or fifteen may be an invaluable member of a Scout troop. On the other hand, those lacking in self-assertion and inclined to shrink from independence should be encouraged to develop self-reliant activities at school and in the home.

Few activities could be better than the Scout Movement for boys at these ages, as it forms an introduction to social duties and responsibilities along lines admirably adapted to the psychology of adolescence. The enthusiasm with which young people fling themselves into group activities at this period (eleven to sixteen years) indicates the need of mind and body for just this sort of development. While games should not be neglected, they need supplementing through modes of expression more explicitly social.

c. SUBLIMATION

Although "the flight from the nest" is bound up with biological-sexual factors, we should never forget that the boy of fourteen or fifteen to seventeen or eighteen years (or even later) is normally *erotic* in his mentality and not *sexual*. (Sex feeling there may be, of course, but it is not yet directed towards a definite person of the other sex.)

The difference is fundamental. To worship from afar, and free from physical desire, is characteristic of this age; and the erotic feeling is as likely (at a certain stage) to be awakened by one of the same sex as by one of the other sex. The *Schwärmerei*[1] of the girl of the early and middle teens is, within limits, perfectly normal and necessary, and should on no account be dubbed "silly." It belongs (as Spranger so eloquently urges, ibid., pp. 80 ff.) to the process of spiritual awakening and inward growth; it is a vital phase in the reconstruction of the child-mind and its attachment to outward reality. If it be too severely checked there is a real danger of emotional impoverishment. To encourage girls to devote themselves to cricket or tennis, in order to prevent them becoming "silly," is to nip their budding erotic feeling (the forerunner of healthy sexuality) in the bud, and produce a cold and arrested type. (Cf. Dr. Crichton-Miller, *The New Psychology and the Parent*, p. 104.)

The same applies, in a somewhat different sense, to boys. It is often of great value for the development of manhood that a phase of emotional attraction towards an older man or boy should be passed through. At this stage of development the libido is not definitely focused upon the opposite sex. It has first to play its part in a process of mental ripening, which, in the higher civilisations, is preliminary to physical sexuality.[2] All these

[1] Exalted sentimentality.

[2] "It is only when exaggerated or prolonged that we look upon any homo-sexual phase in adolescence with any misgiving or regard it in any way as having a morbid aspect—such an element commonly

points of view are of thoroughly fundamental significance for sexual education.

During adolescence a large part of the available sex energy (some of it is not available, being tied to the basic instinct) should undergo sublimation and thus help to build up personality. The squandering of this energy in actual sex intercourse during these critical formative years is apt to cause an arrest of mental and emotional life.[1]

The matter has been well put by J. H. Badley (*The Will to Live*, p. 232), ". . . by using their energy in other channels than those of sex alone, sex impulses, so far from conflicting with higher aims, can be made to subserve them and add to the worth as well as the happiness of life. . . . although the needs of sex may be met by giving them their place among the normal

exists without any necessary overt actions and is to some extent a natural phase of development." (Dr. Stanford Read, *The Struggles of Male Adolescence*, pp. 150–2.) It is, however, of great importance that the libido should not acquire a fixation in this direction.

[1] The question will, of course, be asked, "What about masturbation?" The old-fashioned idea of the enormous harmfulness of this habit is no longer held; that at one time or another nearly all boys and girls practise it is now admitted. Normally, the development of new interests causes it to be dropped. But if much sex energy be squandered in this way (especially in later adolescence) the habit will obviously tend to prevent sublimation, and in this way is harmful, even if we do not now regard it from such a sinister standpoint. The reader cannot do better than consult *The Struggles of Male Adolescence* on this difficult matter; from chap. x I take the following passage: "There is, perhaps, a tendency nowadays to stress the harmlessness of masturbation in just as much an exaggerated degree as its harmfulness used to be impressed upon us by an earlier school. The truth probably lies in taking a midway course." In cases where a parent or guardian suspects real danger due to this matter or to homo-sexual practices, he should at once consult a competent psycho-therapeutic specialist.

experiences and responsibilities of life—this is the ideal of marriage—even this solution does not cover the whole range of the sex life or all its possibilities. There must still be times, both in marriage and outside it—in adolescence, for example, when the urge first awakens—when immediate satisfaction is inadvisable. And when the direct and immediate satisfaction of an instinct cannot be found, its energy is only too likely . . . either to be dammed back until it bursts the barrier in a harmful flood, or else to spend itself in painful conflict, which may lead to serious harm to mind and body, unless it can find an outlet through some other channel in which it can be useful to the individual and the community. The finding of such outlets, and the substitution of a 'higher' for a 'lower' mode of response, is the process of sublimation. It is indeed thanks to this process that man has advanced beyond the animals not merely in mastery of his surroundings but in spiritual growth." Mr. Badley then goes on to point out that imagination is in this work more important than will, for "whatever is vividly present in imagination tends to express itself in outward action. It is advisable, therefore, to enlist imagination on the side of activities that can thus be shaped into strongly held interests and ideals; for, if left at the service of instinctive impulses, imagination is sure to prove a stronger force than either reason or will." (The reader is also referred to Tansley's *The New Psychology*, chap. vii.)

d. LOVE AND FRIENDSHIP

It will thus be seen that the erotic and the sexual are, in a sense, opposite poles during this phase of development;

their union in actual sex love is not possible until a later age.

It is, in civilised races, quite normal that sex, on its physical side, should be held back while the libido—the psychic energy attached to the impulse—should be set free (partially) for an energising of the higher mental and emotional centres. (In the case of many primitive tribes, where boys and girls begin to practise sex intercourse in their early teens, these centres simply remain atrophied.)[1]

"The repression and sublimation of the sex impulse during childhood and youth is an essential condition for the development and maintenance in any society of a high level of culture. And of such repression and sublimation respect of the boy for woman is the principal condition." This weighty passage from McDougall's *Social Psychology* (21st ed., pp. 358–9) is specially to be recommended to the notice of those superficial would-be "advanced" writers (often youthful feminists) who see the solution of the problems of youth in teaching half-baked boys and immature girls the arts of contraception—this path leads to cultural and moral bankruptcy.

It is just at this period—say from sixteen to twenty—that the flood of new energy furnished by the ripening of sex should be poured into the channels of the higher self, fertilising the rich fields of art, literature, science, and social and cultural life. From this standpoint the one-sided sublimation of sex through sport is open to severe criticism. The mere "working-off" of the superfluous sex energy by means of hard exercise in the open air may detract attention from less desirable forms of

[1] On this matter the reader may well consult McDougall's *Social Psychology* (chap. "Sex Instinct").

activity, but it may (and very often does) cause culturally more valuable centres to perish through starvation. It remains for the wise teacher or parent to find the golden mean. To say to the adolescent who is found brooding over poetry or writing love-letters, "Come along and play football, then you'll forget these unwholesome ideas!" is to come perilously near barbarism.

In chapter iv of Spranger's above-mentioned work we have a most illuminating treatment of the vital connection between youthful eroticism and the imaginative and idealistic aspects of personality. The whole fabric of human faith and idealism is, he maintains, linked up immediately with the erotic phase of adolescence, the seed-time of vision. This "mental blossoming" is "decisive for the depth of the whole future development" (p. 98). Then it is that the "form-giving, upward-striving cosmic forces" permeate the personality (p. 104).[1]

On p. 98 Spranger utters a special warning of the danger to boys (even more than to girls) of trivial love-making and cheap flirtations at this age. Erotic idealism is productive, while passing flirtations and the frequenting (overmuch) of dances and so forth distract the mind from deeper interests. The creative forces of personality should at this age ripen slowly in the depths of the mind.

Much of the foregoing, I know very well, will strike the reader (if he is typically "modern") as being too idealistic or even romantic. The question is how far we should allow ourselves to be dominated by what is possibly no more than a passing reaction against all deep

[1] Bearing this in mind, it appears very questionable whether it is wise to give sex instruction (at any rate to older boys and girls) in the matter-of-fact spirit now usually recommended, since we thus do our best to destroy the glamour of sex, which to the adolescent is quite natural and of definite developmental value.

feeling and sentiment. Are we so sure that we really desire a world stripped of romance and idealism?

The development of those areas of personality which are closely linked with the sex instinct is a process involving some risks—that cannot be denied—but the old tag "nothing venture nothing have" is valid in this field. To play for safety by leaving sex on one side and seeking to destroy its mystery and power by means of unsentimental comradeship between boys and girls (or, to take a more extreme case, by means of the nudity cult, which would render young people immune by letting them mingle together naked) is at the same time to forgo the immensely significant enrichments of personality which are correlated with the sex instinct in its sublimated forms.

. . . . .

Every educator is aware of the great educational value of *friendship*. To the adolescent it is essential that his personality should be defined by contact with other personalities. The arguments, the endless exchanges of ideas, and the quarrels of juvenile friendship make up a phase of development.

As Hoffmann truly observes (*Die Reifezeit*, chap. iv), the continual search for the ideal friend, despite all the bitter disappointment that so often goes with it, is a vital part of self-realisation. The boy probably never finds the harmonious relationship for which he craves, but the reactions between the "ego" and the "other" help his self-feeling to ripen. "The choice of the friend is of decisive importance for the future mental and emotional development. The unfavourable consequences of wrong friendships are generally recognised. In the case of the girl who 'goes wrong,' it is a regular rule that a girl friend has started her on her downward track."

Spranger asks the question: "What is of really decisive importance in the moral development of the adolescent?" and answers it as follows: "The *one* person to whom the adolescent devotes himself with his whole *Lebensglaube* (belief in life)." He longs to be understood, and through this understanding he "forms himself." The inner life of the adolescent (continues Spranger) is a chaos of unformed feelings and tendencies, and in order to achieve an inner unity he must seek to form himself for a time upon someone else, preferably, of course, a riper (but not *too* ripe) personality. He does not unaided attain to clarity as to his own nature. Ideas or moral imperatives cannot do this. "Personality can only acquire form through that which is itself personality and form." "No error of youth," says Spranger, "is so great as the idea that he is, or can be, free from authority." An outwardly imposed authority may be scorned, but he yearns, often with passionate intensity, for an inwardly recognised authority.

It may be useful to remark, in passing, that the New Psychology, too, does not (as many seem to think) make entirely in the direction of freedom and indiscipline. (The reader is advised on this point to follow the important argument of Dr. Hadfield in *Psychology and Morals*.)

The time when the much idealised friend or teacher is found to be but ordinary flesh and blood may be so hard as to bring about a temporary crisis; but a stage of development has been achieved and that is all that really matters.

e. THE CRITICAL STAGE OF ADOLESCENCE

It is thus clear that the entire problem of sex development is a question of stages.

What is normal at one stage becomes abnormal at another. The remote and romantic attitude towards the girl of the unspoiled boy of seventeen is the right mentality for that stage, because it holds him back from premature and degrading associations; but at a later stage a more realistic attitude is needful if an arrest is not to be produced. There are, of course, no sharp divisions. The idealism of the adolescent is mixed with physical desire, even if the latter is vague and held in check by subconscious forces; and the realism of the mature should not involve the total loss of idealism. But the boyishly sentimental attitude towards women of a certain type of western man is a sign of arrested development, of a prolongation of the psychology of adolescence into later years.

It is necessary to lay some weight upon these points since one of the major dangers of present-day education is the undue curtailment of the period of ripening which lies between *physical* and *mental* maturity. So obvious are the factors making for this result that it is hardly needful to enumerate them. The reading of unsuitable literature, the cinema, the conversation of elders or of precocious schoolmates, unwisdom on the part of the parents, a type of sex instruction which is too matter-of-fact and goes too far—all these things tend to kill the tender shoots of boyish idealism, or to force them into premature growth. We return to sex instruction later; it is sufficient to point out here that it must, above all things, be graded with reference to the stages of development.

Of very great psychological importance is the rôle played by *curiosity* in the advance from one stage to the next. The function of the wise parent and teacher is to keep this curiosity alive, guarding on the one hand against repression and on the other against killing it through a too complete "enlightenment." A certain degree of curiosity about "the facts of life" is natural to a boy of (say) twelve to sixteen years of age and is a subconscious impetus to work and study (cf. p. 124).

. . . . .

It is not difficult to see that such considerations as the foregoing go to make up a powerful case for *an advance in the age of school attendance*. The extraordinarily critical nature of this period (especially of the years fourteen to sixteen) makes it most undesirable that the boy or girl should be flung haphazard into the world to pick up his life-knowledge from factory mates, the popular Press, and the cinema.

This matter has been dealt with by Dr. Olive Wheeler, of University College, Cardiff, in her work *Youth* (University of London Press). In the section entitled "The Critical Nature of Adolescence," she says: "The only policy that meets the psychological facts is that of primary education for all children, and secondary education for all adolescents, at least during the time of greatest instability." To give the first without the second "is as though a gardener were to tend his plants until the buds appear, only to pluck them up by the roots in order to avoid the additional expense that would be involved in continuing their cultivation to the fruit-bearing stage!"

It would hardly be too much to say that this matter of the prolongation of adolescence, of the due ripening of the mental and emotional personality in the period between puberty and maturity, is the central problem of education (at any rate in its later stages). There, too, lies the key to the very difficult problem of bridging the gulf between the generations with which we were concerned in Chapter III.

"The height to which the mental development will ascend seems to me to be related to the duration of this period," writes Hoffmann (*Die Reifezeit*, p. 243). So much depends, he explains, upon the *geistige Austrahlung* of the biological function of sex.

f. THE MASCULINE PHASE

The problem of education in relation to sex is thus largely a matter of retarding the physical expression of sex until the personality as a whole has had time to ripen.

Friendship, school-work, sport, social life, group activities (e.g. boy scouts, girl guides, clubs)—all these and many other factors can play a large part in providing channels of self-expression. In the absence of such interests direct physical manifestations of sex are much more likely.

A close contact between the boy and an older personality of the same sex is a vital factor in the development of the mind and body. The early years of the boy have normally been spent under female authority, and it is essential that the male element should predominate when he comes to leave home. Otherwise the mother-fixation is liable to be transformed into a substitute mother-fixation in relation to a woman teacher. A phase of revolt against the female and aspiration towards manhood under masculine inspiration is one of the stages which must be passed through on the path of development. The boy must find himself as a boy before he can fruitfully make contact with the opposite sex.

Nowhere is this vital matter of the stages of boyish development more sharply emphasized than in Dr. Crichton-Miller's little book, *The New Psychology and the Parent*, where he makes a division as follows:

0–8 first feminine phase (mother period).
8–12 first masculine phase (father period).
12–18 second masculine phase (school period).
18 onwards, second feminine phase (mating period).

Although, of course, purely schematic, these divisions will be found valuable as a definite indication of the stages of healthy male development. Any marked variation from this time-table will be dangerous to normal development. At about the age of eight the impingement of definitely masculine psychic forces upon the growing mind is essential to the liberation of the latent male faculties. This is not, as is supposed by many, a mere question of "hardening" the boy. Men teachers are by no means necessarily hardier in their life-outlook and practice than female. The whole problem goes much deeper than this. The male influence belongs to *the process of self-formation and self-realisation*, by which the boy transcends his amorphous infantile mentality and crosses the gap between childhood and the world of reality. If it be said: Why cannot a woman teacher help him across? the answer is, because the child will inevitably (even if quite unconsciously) identify the woman teacher with his mother, and react towards her in the same way.[1] His own independent development can thus

[1] See the quotation from Dr. Stanford Read on p. 132.

be secured only under competent male guidance. The woman is the life-giver; but the man is the form-giver.

There must be no misunderstanding. Not for a moment does such a statement as this reflect upon the woman teacher or upon women in general. Female influence is vital to male development. But the years when it is fruitfully exercised are (speaking roughly) those before eight and after eighteen. The boy himself does not want it during the period of "flight from the nest."[1]

If the boy, as Schiller wrote, "draws proudly away from the girl" in this period, that does not imply any contempt for the feminine. He does so in response to a deep inner necessity of his being. He is subconsciously making himself more fit for an ultimate union of two completed personalities. It is much to be regretted that a totally false and superficial notion of what is really possible in the way of sex equality has led many parents and teachers to overlook the necessity for these stages in the great process of self-realisation. They are accepted, however, by all who are acquainted with the truths of modern psychology.

g. THE EGO AND THE WORLD

The foregoing sketch of development is based upon the idea of completion, of that enlargement of the self, that

[1] The issues involved in this problem have been much obscured by the use of crude physical standards. Thus, a certain journal recently argued as if the fact that boys who are educated chiefly by women can prove themselves equal at football to boys educated under men completely settled the whole question! What a naïve materialism lies behind this assumption! One of the chief functions of the educator is precisely to enable boys to transcend that stage of development when sport and athletics seem all-important.

becoming *mature* which has already been emphasized in the first chapter of this work.

Does this suggest an ego-centric view of psychology? The answer is, No. Because the individual is essentially social in the sense that *in vacuo* he cannot develop at all. The very first condition of maturity is the transcendence of the narrow if innocent ego-centricity that is the mark of childhood. (From this point of view we may regard the gospel of self-centred individualism preached by the "advanced" as a species of arrested development; it is the creed of those who do not *want* to outgrow childhood, often by reason of a secret fear of adult life.)

Towards the close of Chapter III it was explained that the growth to maturity of a civilised (as distinct from a barbaric) personality is brought about by a synthesis of freedom and authority.[1] The form-giving power of social and cultural norms is essential to development; in their absence the mind of youth remains a mere chaos of shapeless impulses and vague emotions. The peculiar difficulty of the present-day situation is that we stand in between a world of decaying forms and a new world of forms not yet perceived. More than twenty years ago our greatest danger—an arrest in development due to a failure to cross successfully the gap between childhood and adult life—was very clearly foreseen by Dr. Stanley Hall.

To a certain large school of thought in the educational world becoming mature is no more than a "natural"

[1] The problem of authority and freedom in education is treated with unrivalled force and clarity by Dr. Foerster in his works *Autorität und Freiheit* (pub. Kösel in Munich) and *Schule und Charakter* (pub. Schulthess in Zurich). In the very useful little book mentioned on p. 22, Dr. Richert, too, has some excellent things to say on this ever-present problem.

process; it follows upon growth, in much the same sense as an increase of weight or the development of hair on the face.

There are many schools of naturalism; but they are alike in failing to realise the true nature of the gulf between the child and the adult—that it is spiritual and not physical.

To the behaviourist a child is simply a lump of matter possessing a somewhat superior power of reflex action, as compared with other lumps, such as jelly-fish or pieces of stone. (When we remember that a distinguished protagonist of this school committed himself to the statement that, given *any* normal baby, he could at will transform it into a labourer, a poet, a musician, or a great statesman, we can form some idea of the complete passivity with which this school regards human nature as being endowed!)

Inevitably, to those who think like this, growing up is simply allowing the lump in question to swell a little bigger. The problem of the *ego* and the world is non-existent, *for all is world and there is no ego*! If, paradoxically, educational naturalists often make a great fuss about "personality," that is only another example of the confusion in which our concepts are now involved. For there is no room for any such thing within the framework of this view of reality. To be a cog in a vast machine of social and industrial life is all that any given lump can aspire to. Complete subjection to impersonal forces is the sole destiny of humanity.

• • • • •

To those who regard the growth of the child from the psychological (as distinct from the mechanical) standpoint, the relationship between the *ego* and the world is a great problem.

To become mature means to conquer reality. It is a *task* and not an impersonal process. Often, this task demands immense effort, conflict, and sacrifice; both from the subject and from those who are guiding him. To remain a child is, of course, much easier—hence the popularity of the "back-to-childhood" cult (satirised by Wyndham Lewis in *Paleface* and *Time and Western Man*). This and other "backward cults" are explicable upon the view that psychic energy released from a specific concentration flows back along the line of least resistance.

In this conflict it cannot be said that truth lies wholly on either side. Society seeks to mould the child and the child resists. From the standpoint of those who want to destroy society, the child is always right; from the standpoint of orthodoxy, on the other hand, the child tends to be crushed. But it is precisely out of this conflict that reality is won. Society is not a rigid mould into which the child can be forced. But if the child grows up in pure freedom he will never find the reality which lies behind society, for he will remain confined in his narrow self. Each generation can do something to remodel society; but each generation must first learn from society that which it needs for self-completion.

The reforming influences of education, says the Freudian, Ernest Jones, must provoke conflict before their aim can be achieved: "Without them the individual would remain a selfish, jealous, impulsive, aggressive, dirty, immodest, cruel, ego-centric, and conceited animal, inconsiderate to the needs of others, and unmindful of the complicated social and ethical standards that go to make a civilised society." (Quoted by Rusk, *The Philo-*

sophical Bases of Education, p. 121.) (As Dr. Rusk remarks, it is of especial interest to see that the Freudian standpoint, so far from being wholly instinctive, really posits the existence of cultural values as an essential factor in development, even if it does not give us any satisfactory explanation of their genesis.) It is an important truth that, although psycho-analysis seeks to remove conflict, it nevertheless admits the part conflict plays in development—"man is the only animal that develops complexes" (Rusk, p. 124). Thus regarded, the more extreme naturalistic school, which would leave children alone to follow all their impulses, leads to stagnation by destroying the life-giving element of conflict and allowing psychic energy to canalise itself along the line of least resistance.

In a word, "growing up" is not an inevitable process but a flower of civilisation. Remove the pressure of civilisation and children remain fixed on an immature level.[1]

The frontier of the adult world is marked by the birth of *values*—intellectual, moral, aesthetic. The introduction to this world of *Geistesleben*—of super-individual, objective values—is the task of the educator and parent. It is from this standpoint alone that formative power can be brought to bear. In this world personality is created. On the other hand, in the world of passivity, where men and women are so much will-less material in the grip of the machine of modern life, we do not get beyond a species of vegetation.

. . . . .

It is our great difficulty to-day that reality has become problematic. Our values—which form the fulcrum with

[1] A very original and striking treatment of this problem is to be found in *The Art of Being Ruled* (part ix).

which youth can be moved—shift so rapidly that we are made dizzy.

As we saw in the first section, it is the conflict in the field of ultimate realities which above all creates the present insecurity in education and in the whole relationship between youth and the older generation.

All educators are agreed that to bring about a right adjustment between the *ego* and the world is the task of education. But to-day, *what is the world?* There is a Catholic world, a materialistic world, a Christian Science world, a sophistical modern world, and a dozen other worlds. All these have their own private systems of values.

Faced with such a situation, parents and teachers are apt to "let things slide" in a sort of despair. Nevertheless, however much confusion may exist in this respect, we cannot—if we wish to educate at all and to overcome, in any way, the disastrous gulf between the generations—overlook the ultimate problem of values in its relation to youth. When youth is disappointed here the result is revolt against all authority and a mood of rebellion and cynicism.

To bridge for the young the gap (which alone they cannot cross) between immaturity and maturity is the function of authority as represented by parent, school, and college. It must be repeated that the desire of youth is directed towards *growth* and not towards irresponsible freedom. The condition upon which the older generation can retain the respect and confidence of youth is that they should possess values to give to youth. In this way the gulf is bridged, because the growing mind craves intensely for a contact with the new world of objectivity which lies beyond childhood.

This may not be the easiest solution of our problem, but it is the only real solution.

CHAPTER VII

SEX INSTRUCTION

a. AN INDIVIDUAL MATTER
b. SOME PRACTICAL HINTS
c. PSYCHOLOGY OR PROPAGANDA?

a. AN INDIVIDUAL MATTER

Those will certainly be disappointed who look to find in this book some easy ready-made path through the thicket of sex instruction. No one but a quack would claim to know of such a path. The whole subject abounds with difficulties. Leading authorities are far from agreeing as to aims and methods.

If we leave children alone and shrink from the responsibility of enlightening them, there is always the danger that they may pick up harmful and misleading knowledge. Early ideas of this kind, crude, fantastic, and obscene as they often are, do immense harm, in many cases sinking down into the subconscious mind to emerge later on in life as a horror of the sexual (or perhaps as a stimulus to premature sexuality).

Thus a girl of thirteen was first enlightened as to the facts of sex by an older companion, who told her how she had hidden herself in the cupboard in her parents' bedroom in order to observe what went on, and proceeded to relate a highly fantastic story based upon this experience. This made such an impression upon the younger girl that she retained till past the age of twenty a strong sentiment of disgust towards everything connected with sexual life.

On the other hand, there is the opposite danger that by telling children too much we may lead them to concentrate their minds unduly upon this side of life. It is, moreover, extremely easy to think that we have "explained" something when the child has not, in reality, understood at all, so that even after careful instruction he may form the wildest ideas on sexual matters.

Spranger tells us how two little girls, who had been very much "enlightened" and had in addition enlarged their knowledge by a study of the encyclopaedia, conceived the quite imaginary idea that their governess was carrying on an illicit love affair and anticipated a baby; they immediately wrote her an anonymous letter in which they explained how she might evade her troubles by the use of means of abortion!

It is the difficult task of the parent or teacher to sail the narrow channel between Scylla and Charybdis; on either side are perilous rocks.

Above all, this is *an individual problem*. What may help one child may be quite the wrong thing for another. It is, however, fairly safe to say that where there is a sign of true curiosity—as distinct from a mere random asking of questions—some accurate information should be given. But not more than the child in question is likely to assimilate, as judged by age, general intelligence, and previous knowledge.

The extreme difficulty of dealing with sex instruction *en masse* is clear when we consider how very wide apart are the real ages (as measured by degree of maturity) in a class of approximately equal nominal ages. If we take a boys' class of fourteen years, the majority will be in a pubescent state, but some may be already through the crisis, while a few slowly developing types may still be pre-pubescent children.

Instruction suitable for the first of these groups is already too late for the second group and too soon for the third!

It is thus understandable that the majority of experienced educators are opposed to class-teaching of this difficult subject (see p. 122). Those who favour it are for the most part theorists, who mean very well but are not sufficiently acquainted with the real psychology of boys and girls.

b. SOME PRACTICAL HINTS

The general scheme of sex instruction is indicated by the stages of development referred to on p. 111.

There is almost complete unanimity amongst psychologists that the first enlightenment should come from the mother during the earliest stage (up to eight years). It is ideal when the child's own observations (for example, when the cat has kittens) can be used as the basis of a few very simple explanations, which need not go beyond what the child wants to know, and should, of course, be kept strictly within the limits of what he seems able to understand.

The actual growth of a child in the womb is a fact apparently quite beyond the grasp of young children (see the examples of children's reactions to sex instruction in Dr. Piaget's book, *The Child's Conception of the World*).

They usually want to know "where babies come from," taking it for granted (almost, if not quite invariably) that they are ready-made. More than the general idea that babies come from the mother cannot usually be assimilated by young children. There will be no occasion to refer to the father's part, about which there is no curiosity (in a sexual sense) at this age. In any case, it would (save, perhaps, in rare cases) be incomprehensible; and it is undesirable to attract attention to facts beyond the normal mental range of this age.

How far the mother should actually go during this first phase is individual. In the case of precocious children who show a great deal of curiosity it may be necessary to answer innumerable questions and to give more information than would be at all advisable with a less forward child. But even in such cases it must not be assumed that the child will really *understand* facts lying beyond its stage of development, however much curiosity may be exhibited.

Late childhood—from eight or nine until twelve—is marked, for boys, by a turning towards the father. Further instruction, beyond that given by the mother earlier, is not always necessary during this phase (in which interest does not usually turn specially towards matters related to sex), but if, owing to special curiosity or a danger of acquiring impure knowledge from companions or otherwise, more enlightenment seems advisable, it should come from the father, and should prepare the way for the fuller instruction which the near approach of puberty makes desirable.

In the school, carefully graded teaching on animal and plant life may be useful as leading up to sex enlightenment, but it is best (in the opinion of most psychologists) that such teaching should touch upon sex *incidentally* rather than focus attention upon it specifically. It is all to the good if knowledge relating to sex can be absorbed naturally, without making a fuss about it.

* * * * *

It is not, of course, possible to say at what age the more precise instruction corresponding to the advent of puberty, with its special problems, should be given. Much discrimination should be used by the parent or teacher who is chiefly responsible for the boy's development. Owing to the extreme shyness of many types, it is hard to tell whether the boy is pondering over sexual difficulties or not. At this age the boy who shows no signs of special interest in sex matters may be the very one who most needs help. At no period of development, probably, is the need for sympathy and understanding between children and parents so evident as at this time. Twelve may, for some types, not be too soon for more detailed knowledge. With others, fourteen, fifteen, or even sixteen may be soon enough. It must be remembered that knowledge given too soon may be unassimilated and almost useless.

In *A Text Book of Sex Instruction* (p. 209 f.) Mr. Gallichan gives the views of a number of eminent educationists on the subject of sex instruction. Nearly the whole weight of this opinion is against class instruction.

Thus Mr. Badley, the well-known head of Bedales, after explaining that he does not trust much to sermons or general talks, says: "I attach far more value to a good talk with the boy alone at the age of fourteen or fifteen (I assume that this is not the first time he has been talked with, but I should wish it to be by his parents—his mother especially—before he comes to school and in the earlier years there), a talk which will make it easy for him to come and talk again if he wants to, and another before he leaves school on the new conditions and dangers he will then meet." At the same time (he adds) some mention of sex matters in class-work may be useful, if only in removing the mistaken sense of shame and the feeling of "stolen waters" which do so much harm.

It must be repeated that sex instruction is a highly individual matter. There can be no such thing as a rigid scheme of instruction suitable for all boys or girls, even of a given age. Everything depends on personality and character-forming influences.

c. PSYCHOLOGY OR PROPAGANDA?

It is probable that, at the present day, the tendency is to give too much rather than too little sex instruction. The pendulum has swung a little too far to the "left."

The German pedagogical psychologist, F. W. Foerster (chiefly known as the author of *Jugendlehre*), considers that a too early explanation of sexual matters, especially in the case of the modern child, is liable to lead to premature development: "The dangers of impure knowledge being acquired unknown to the parents are best met by a careful all-round education, by an intimate relationship between parents and children, and by the cultivation of the sense of shame." (*Marriage and the Sex Problem*, p. 193.)

On the other hand, the "left-wing" of the sex-reform school believes (apparently) that one cannot have too much instruction or give it too soon. It should be stated definitely that such views as these have nothing to do with a genuine study of childhood and youth—they form part of the "politicisation of sex," the popular anti-Christian and anti-morality propaganda of the circles referred to in Chapter XII. The whole weight of up-to-date informed opinion is behind the idea that sex instruction should follow development and not anticipate it. In reality this is the only possible school of thought from a strictly psychological viewpoint, since the child cannot genuinely understand what lies beyond the stage of growth—physical and mental—at which he has arrived, and merely to cram him with undigested information is unwholesomely stimulating, if he takes any interest in it at all![1]

There is, further, the important point that an explanation of sex life in advance of development, by anticipating curiosity, tends to kill one of the main incentives to development. (Cf. Dr. Foerster, *Marriage and the Sex Problem*, chap. vii.)[2]

. . . . .

Considerations of space make it impossible for me to dwell upon the very interesting contributions of Spranger and Hoffmann to our problem. Their position represents a reaction against the "tell-everything" school, and is based upon a very detailed study of child psychology and of actual case material. Spranger specially stresses the futility of a purely intellectual enlightenment; where strong, deep-seated racial passion is in question, mere abstract knowledge is of little avail. A wise all-round development of the boy or girl is the one safe goal.

[1] Dr. Read (*Struggles of Male Adolescence*, p. 69) emphasises the extreme difficulty of real understanding on the part of the young, since "even when imparted adequately by the right person" it must "remain abstract in nature."

[2] On p. 194 of the above-mentioned work, Foerster quotes Dr. Stelzel, the psycho-therapist, on sex instruction: "The best method is that . . . the parents should introduce references to matters connected with sex into their conversation, as a matter of course, without leading the children to regard the subject as in any way peculiar." But premature enlightenment, Dr. Stelzel continues, "would involve a great injury to the development of humanity" on account of this anticipation.

Youth contains within itself the antidote to sex danger if the educator knows how to use it, says Spranger. This is perhaps the very core of the whole problem. There is in the unspoiled boy or girl a profound natural instinct of purity and modesty. Those who deny this speak as doctrinaires, and not as scientific students—everyone who knows real boys or girls must be struck by the often surprising power of this instinct. This is the *true* as distinct from the *false* sense of shame. There is (in Dr. Foerster's opinion) a very grave danger that this inward feeling for chastity may be injured by a too explicit dwelling upon sex matters in class teaching or otherwise.[1]

Most educators will perhaps not go so far as Foerster (who represents "right-wing" opinion) in this direction, but there can be no doubt that an immense amount of harm is done by those who advocate sex enlightenment, not as a genuine pedagogical method, but simply as a weapon in the war against marriage and monogamy. In most of the works of the left-wing school of sex reformers it is perfectly clear that they envisage sex instruction, not as a preparation for marriage, but as an introduction to sexual promiscuity. To "moderns" of this school all shame, without distinction, comes under the head of

[1] McDougall says: "It is too often assumed that mere knowledge of the facts of sex and of what is most desirable and admirable in the conduct of the sex life is all-important and all-sufficient. But knowledge may be more dangerous than ignorance; ignorance of some of the facts is a great and necessary safeguard of youth; a second-hand familiarity with the facts of sexual vice cannot fail to be injurious to youth, and even a full insight into the psychology of sex is highly dangerous." McDougall then remarks upon the fact that medical students, in spite of their great familiarity with all the evils of sexual laxity, are in no way distinguished for greater wisdom in conduct! (*Social Psychology*, 21st ed., p. 360.)

"false shame"; the object is to remove altogether the taboos and inhibitions which now stand between the adolescent and immediate sex gratification. (The argument running: "But there is nothing to be ashamed of in sex, which is a pure and holy thing, therefore shame is all humbug," is utterly superficial. It could be used only by those who cannot distinguish between true and false shame. The former protects sex from cheapness and degradation; the latter is the mask of prurience.)

Boys and girls enlightened in this fashion can hardly fail to think: "Now we have finished with the theory, let us get on to the practice!" For there is here no realisation whatever of the important educational rôle played by shame, modesty, chastity, or even self-control. The true sense of shame, which serves to counterbalance the force of the sex impulse and allows the latter time to ripen, has performed for thousands of years a valuable service in the evolution of the higher races—the absurd notion that it is nothing but a fruit of modern Puritanism (or even of Christianity at all) could never be entertained by any well-informed person; it is a mere trick of propaganda.

There can be no doubt, as Spranger says, that a true sense of shame belongs to the mental structure of the higher races, and quite apart from the difficult problem of how it may have originated must be taken into account by those who have to deal with youth.

From an educational standpoint sex instruction can only be regarded as a branch of character-building as a whole. It would be difficult to improve upon the saying of Spranger that if the teacher or parent wants to help the adolescent to overcome his sex difficulties, he "must tackle the building-up of the whole soul, the strengthening of the idealistic and ethical elements. Only a definite soul-form, in which all forces are consolidated to a system in a hierarchy of values, is a protection to youth in sex difficulties. This is not moralising; it is the statement of a purely psychological fact, since the soul is to be regarded as a structure whose development is guided by a form-giving principle." (*Die Psychologie des Jugendalters*, p. 139.)

BIBLIOGRAPHICAL NOTE

The following works—representing highly divergent points of view—will be found valuable to the student of the Sex Instruction Question:

HAVELOCK ELLIS. *Studies in the Psychology of Sex.* (Especially vol. vi.) *Man and Woman.*

FOREL, A. *The Sexual Question.*

STANLEY HALL. *Adolescence.*

MICHEL, PROF. *Sexual Ethics.*

BIGELOW, M. *Sex Education.*

LYTTELTON, CANON. *Training of the Young in the Laws of Sex.*

CHADWICK, MARY. *Difficulties in Child-Development*

The New Generation. (Section 5.)

CLASSEN, DR. *Studien zur Sexualpsychologie und Pädagogik der Gegenwart.* (Pub. Beyer in Langensalza). (A valuable up-to-date survey of the Sex Instruction Question, with bibliography of German works.)

STERN, DR. E. *Die Erziehung und die Sexuelle Frage.* (Berlin, 1927.)

FOERSTER, DR. F. W. *Religion und Charakterbildung.*

MOLL, A. *Das Sexualleben des Kindes.* (Trans. as "The Sexual Life of Children.")

Einführung in die Sexualpädagogik. (Lectures. Pub. *Zentral-Institut,* Berlin.)

PART III

SPECIAL PROBLEMS

CHAPTER VIII

SEX AND THE TEACHER

a. MEN TEACHERS FOR BOYS
b. THE NEED FOR SEX EQUALITY

a. MEN TEACHERS FOR BOYS

The foregoing chapters have made abundantly clear the central importance of *personality* for the whole work of education.

The view of education as a mere assimilation of facts is now definitely out-of-date.

We have seen how the growth of the child (especially in an emotional sense) is dependent upon the personal influences—parent, friend, teacher—which are brought to bear upon the unfolding mind. For the boy (see p. 110) an authoritative male influence, in the critical years between about eight and seventeen or eighteen, is of decisive importance. I must repeat that this has nothing to do with any crude ideas of "he-mannism," or of mere physical hardening, or training in sports. Competent masculine guidance is far more vital from a purely psychological and spiritual point of view than it is from the physical standpoint.

In view of this important truth it is well that we should examine with some care the present condition of education in England. In 1854, 63 per cent of elementary school teachers were men, while in 1931 the proportion was no more than 26 per cent. This means that large numbers of boys are now taught by women (in fact, some 225,000). (Further details will be found on p. 141.)

We are travelling along the road that leads to the American system, where women are almost completely dominant in the field of primary instruction. At the present critical time—when the economic situation makes it increasingly difficult to obtain the right type of man—it is of vital importance that *we should maintain the principle of sex equality in the teaching profession.*

. . . . .

Although, to those who are in touch with present-day psychology, further confirmation of the above point of view will hardly appear necessary, it will be of interest to the general reader to quote the views of two or three recognised authorities.

Dr. Stanford Read (a leading psychologist of the modern school; lecturer in psychology to the Royal Bethlehem Hospital; and author of *The Struggles of Male Adolescence*) has been good enough to write the following summary of his views specially for this book:

"Most certainly, I fully endorse your opinion that only men teachers should be employed for boys in their adolescent stage. There are many psychological reasons why this should be so. School life is the first important step which moulds the instinctive life of the boy in the direction of that outer and larger world to which eventually he must adapt, away from the narrow confines of emotional parental and family sway. We know only too well that the greatest factors which will tend towards the evolution of a stable personality involve freedom from undue maternal fixations. The teacher in the school, representing authority, is a parental surrogate, and if this teacher is a woman, the youth is unconsciously led to react to her on an infantile emotional plane. In the natural unfolding of a boy's mental growth after the age of nine years, identification with the father gradually becomes a potent force, contributing largely to the formation of his ideal self. Thus, a man teacher, who is necessarily a father-substitute—through the boy's tendencies to imitate and be suggestible towards him—can call forth the desire to learn and win approval. It will mainly be through such an influence that the attributes of self-reliance and manliness will be adequately established and organised."

The views of Dr. Crichton-Miller, one of the foremost authorities in England, have already been put before the reader.

Another noteworthy opinion is that of Mr. Ernest Barker (late Principal of King's College), who states that: "Education is very largely a matter of personality; much—very much—depends on the impression which the personality of the teacher can make and the suggestion which it can convey. The influence of masculine personality is an essential condition of the successful education of boys. Women are the most conscientious and painstaking of teachers. It is not their fault that they are not men and cannot exert the sort of influence which men can exercise; it is part of the order of nature. One cannot fly in the face of that order."

It is, I need hardly say, not a matter of a few individual opinions but of the whole trend of modern psychology. No one acquainted with the work of Freud and Jung, for example, could doubt the central importance of the intangible psychic forces bound up with the subconscious life of the parent and teacher (and themselves so intimately related to sex) in the work of forming the life of boys and girls. Not to realise this is to remain in the thought-world of more than twenty years ago.

. . . . .

It should, perhaps, be added that it is not from the standpoint of the New Psychology alone that we arrive at these conclusions as to the importance of the male teacher. Dr. F. W. Foerster (see p. 123), who is widely known as an opponent of Freudian ideas, recently expressed the opinion (in the course of conversation on this matter) that nothing but the prevalence of a mechanical and unpsychological life-outlook could possibly account for the notion that women could, or should, be placed in authority over boys. Discipline, mental and moral, and indeed the whole course of character-building, is bound up with specifically masculine psychic forces (especially, in his opinion, from ten onwards), and it is "a pure absurdity" to entertain the idea of interchangeability between the sexes in the teaching profession (as if training the young were a matter of automatic die-stamping!).

In the sections devoted to *the cult of the child*, and to *the dominance of women*, in *America Set Free*, Keyserling tells us how close is the connection between the almost complete ascendancy of woman in the American social and educational system and what he calls the "infantilism" of the man, the general prevalence of the active, sport-loving, "go-getting" but essentially childish and undeveloped type of male satirised by Sinclair Lewis, Mencken, Edith Wharton, and others. In spite of the innumerable delightful qualities of the modern American (hospitality, open-mindedness, chivalry, generosity, and philanthropy, to mention only one or two) it is almost universally recognised by objective observers that Keyserling's criticism is justified; these positive qualities, charming as they often are, cannot hide the mental arrest which characterises large masses of the people.[1] So good an American as Edna Ferber, the novelist, recently said: "The boys and girls going to our universities have absolutely no serious subjects for discussions; all they can talk about is football . . . they are the most beautiful creatures in the world, but *they are only twelve years old permanently*" (my italics). Can we doubt that the

[1] After speaking (p. 312) of the "psychological supremacy" of woman in the States, Keyserling asserts that the dominance of women in the educational field "makes for the development in the American man of such an extraordinary mother-complex that it cannot help leading to a kind of perpetual infantilism," and on p. 282 he says that American men, despite their business energy, "are essentially infantile —they lack precisely those qualities which make a man, as opposed to the child, which is intrinsically neither male nor female, but something particular of its own." On p. 283 he continues: "Now is this really due to an irrational education? It is. The father symbolises the spiritual principle within the child—hence we can easily understand the practical rôle the father should play in the educational scheme. The centres of relationship of the child's own masculine and feminine principles are externalised in the persons of father and mother." Keyserling then explains that the father (and the teacher is the father-substitute, we should not forget) is responsible for the formation of "an original life, built on the foundation of a consciousness of value as opposed to the qualities of the undifferentiated Eros"; further (p. 287), "the father, failing to fulfil his task as a father, and the child remaining a child in consequence, its natural dependence on the mother is increased to the degree that the boy expects from woman everything he would normally expect from the man his senior in age; and this attitude lasts as long as he lives." Finally (p. 291), "What is culturally wrong with America is that it has no sense of values. All values are of the mind and of the spirit. There are no values inherent even in the most delightful qualities of childhood "

arguments advanced in Chapter VI (*f.* and *g.*) of this study have a real bearing upon this tragic situation?[1]

b. THE NEED FOR SEX EQUALITY

It would not be difficult to bring forward further pages of weighty opinions. But the truth is that the preponderance of women teachers in England (and to a far greater degree in the United States) has nothing to do with the psychological and pedagogical problem—which may be regarded as practically settled in the sense set forth above, in other words, in favour of *sex equality*, of an approximate "fifty-fifty" in the proportion of men and women teachers (apart from infant schools, where, as I need hardly say, women are needed).

How, then, has it come about that we have only 26 per cent of men teachers? (In New York some 6½ per cent only.)

It is our misfortune that we have allowed ourselves to lose sight of what was educationally right under the influence of social and economic forces which had nothing to do with the first object of the school system—*the welfare of the children.*

If the educational system had been based upon the principle of *equality of opportunity* as between the sexes, it is obvious that the influx of men would have been approximately equal to the influx of women. A grave error was made in departing from this principle and

[1] Dr. C. W. Kimmins (ex-Chief Inspector for the L.C.C.) tells us that in the United States "the great majority of the more progressive educationalists" believe that the American boy is seriously injured by coming so little in contact with masculine teachers. (*John O'London's Weekly*, May 18, 1929.)

putting into practice rates of pay which bear no reference to *real* (as distinct from abstract and doctrinaire) equality.

The majority of men teachers are married men with wives and children dependent upon their salaries. The majority of women teachers either have no dependents, or, at most, help some mother or sister (a burden which may, of course, fall equally upon a married man *in addition* to his own family!). Apart from exceptions, *the standard male teacher* is a man with from two to five dependents; *the standard female teacher* is the woman with less than one dependent. As a matter of fact, thousands of women teachers live with their parents and are able to retain most of their earnings as pocket-money.

It is rather difficult to reply with patience to those who cry, "Oh, but some women teachers have parents, sisters, or perhaps even husbands dependent upon them!" Such exceptional cases do exist, just as, on the other side, we might discover men teachers with families of five or six children, or supporting both parents in addition to their own families. But to suggest that the *average* woman teacher has two or three persons (or even one) solely dependent upon her is to talk plain nonsense.

True equality of opportunity means that the standard of living and comfort of the average man teacher should be the same as that of the average woman teacher. The teaching profession would then offer to men the same attraction it does to women—which is obviously not now the case!

The present scales give the man teacher less than 25 per cent more pay than it gives to the woman. But the expenses of a man with three dependents are usually more than double those of a woman with (perhaps) a single semi-dependent. It is thus clear that the woman, under existing rates of pay, is (in an average case) anything from 50 to 100 per cent better off. This is not mere theory. It is obvious from a study of facts. Tens of thousands of women teachers are now able to enjoy comforts and luxuries and (what is more important) cultural advantages, such as lectures, travel, books, etc., which are quite beyond the means of the average man teacher with the same training and experience.

The effect of the present system is, in a word, to *depress the man to a lower economic level*, and, as a result, to cause fewer men and (above all) fewer of the most promising types to enter the profession. About this there can really be no dispute.[1]

[1] It has been repeatedly pointed out by eminent educational authorities that the present tendency towards equality in salaries must end by placing teaching in the hands of women. Thus Mr. G. L. Bruce, L.C.C., wrote a few years ago in the *Daily Telegraph*: "We are within sight of American conditions. . . . The immediate effect of attempting to equalise the two salaries is to make the conditions unequal; to give rather more to the woman and much less to the man. The ultimate and not distant effect must be to drive men out of the teaching profession."

In a fairly large elementary school with which I am well acquainted the situation is as follows: Five men teachers, all married (with sixteen dependents); four women teachers (none with any dependents); ratio of salaries about five to four; result, the men have to struggle to make both ends meet, while the four women teachers can all afford to travel abroad and in general to live on a higher scale.

Unfortunately, the active propaganda in favour of (virtual) sex inequality carried on for many years by the feminist organisations has largely blinded the public to the true facts; it is, for example, not generally realised that a woman teacher, with (say) £250 per annum, who can board and lodge herself comfortably for £100 a year, must be elevated into a superior class if her pay be even approximately equal to that of a man who must yearly pay out for house, food, heating and lighting alone nearly £200. In the United States the male teacher is, in many States, on an economic level much lower than that of the navvy or road-sweeper.

The full absurdity of the existing situation becomes apparent when put in the following form. A certificated man, with some nine to ten years' experience, receives about £270 per annum, and a woman with the same number of years' service, £230. (The exact salaries vary somewhat in different districts, but these figures represent the proportions.) In other words, the wife and children of the man are expected to live on £40 a year, although, according to the representations of the women's associations, the £230 paid to the woman is not excessive for a single person.[1] In reality, it would hardly be possible to rate the expense of maintaining a family of three (without reckoning the man himself) at less than £175 to £200. Regarded thus, the married man teacher is underpaid to the extent of, at the very least, some £140. All this on the assumption that the general standard of living and culture is to be the same for both sexes.

. . . . .

Arguing theoretically, it would be possible to arrange a system of family allowances to balance some of the gross inequalities above mentioned; but if such a system were to be large enough in its scope effectively to readjust the extra expenses of a family and place men and women on a level it would be extremely expensive and is therefore, under the existing critical economic conditions, out of the question.

Speaking *practically*, we can only aim at so adjusting

[1] As is well known, the feminist section of the women teachers demand that the woman teacher (even if single and with no dependents) has the right to receive the same pay as a man with a family; in which case the *man teacher's wife* (who being a woman should surely, in feminist eyes, also possess rights) is in the position of being entitled to—*nothing*!

the scales of remuneration that the children's interests shall be placed first, and since these are best served by equality of opportunity (securing in its turn a steady supply of men teachers) this adjustment must raise men's salaries (in the first place those of the married men) to the point at which the heavy extra expenses of the man are balanced and he is placed on the same footing as the woman. (It must be remembered that single men require larger salaries than single women, speaking generally, since they are frequently saving up to get married—the modern girl seldom saves, with this end in view, for in nine cases out of ten she looks forward to being dependent on her husband after marriage.)

. . . . .

Such an impartial authority as *The Times* writes:

"If authorities were allowed to accumulate what in business is known as a reserve for contingencies, and gained the reputation of using it wisely, they would not only encourage good teachers but would also attract good men into the profession. The Burnham Scales have proved to be of great advantage both to the teachers and to the country; but they have had at least one bad effect. Nearly three-fourths of the teachers in Government service in this country are women, and the proportion of men teachers is decreasing year by year. This tendency is undoubtedly encouraged by the Burnham Scales, under which women are paid roughly four-fifths of the salaries paid to men. Whether women are paid too generously in view of their admittedly lesser responsibilities is one of the subjects to be settled by the committee about to be formed; but it is clear that the present scales are ceasing to attract men into the profession.

After a certain age boys are most effectively taught by men, and it would be most unfortunate if the present low proportion of men to women in the profession were allowed to grow less" (April 10, 1931).

It is a pity that such figures as the following are not widely known and their full weight more appreciated:

In 1930 there were (in England and Wales) 43,000 men teachers and 125,000 women; and the number of children on the register was, infants of 3 to 7, 1,287,000; girls of 7 to 16, 2,090,000; and boys (7–16), 2,144,000.

The Board of Education figures show that, of boys between 7 and 11, no fewer than 5,300 classes were taken by women teachers (only 4 classes of girls were taken by men), and 66,000 mixed classes were under women (1,500 under men).

In the medium category (described as "under and over eleven"), one girls' class was in charge of a man, and nearly 900 boys' classes in charge of women; and even amongst the older boys, in the 11–16 group, no less than 266 boys' classes were under women and 3,700 mixed classes.

It is only necessary to glance at these figures to realise that we are indeed well on the way to the American plan of an educational system run by women.

. . . . .

The whole situation illustrates vividly enough the results in practice of a purely abstract and doctrinaire view of the sex-equality problem. To the simple-minded a "dead-level" sex equality seems good enough. They do not penetrate to the realities underlying the surface. They are not able to perceive that if women, who are free from the special liabilities which law and custom place upon the shoulders of the man, are paid at the same rate as men, this creates a situation that is the negation of equality. In practice it has the effect of immediately placing the woman in a superior position. To those who are so innocent as to take the "dead-level" view of the problem it will seem (for example) that to pay a married woman worker the same salary as that paid to her husband is "equality." Entirely overlooked is the vital fact that the husband alone is responsible (in law and custom) for the upkeep of the home, even although the wife is earning an equal sum of money. Were the campaign for this sort of "equality" accompanied by proposals for relieving husbands from their legal liabilities, it would be easier to believe in the good faith of those who are responsible for it.[1]

The real truth of this matter is that (although many feminists as individuals are quite innocent of such a purpose) the whole movement in favour of a purely outward and formal (as distinct from a real) sex equality is aimed at securing for women the same position of dominance which they possess in the United States (see p. 209). Since the general public is not able to distinguish between genuine equality and a state of affairs in which women have the same rights and the same pay as men, but are free from some of the most important masculine responsibilities and financial burdens, it should be fairly easy for this aim to be achieved.

[1] The utterly farcical situations which result from this sort of "equality" are illustrated by such a case as this: Mrs. A. is living apart from her husband, who pays her £100 per annum separation allowance (out of his teacher's income of £300); at the same time she earns, as a teacher, £260 per annum—her income is thus £360 (under the feminist regime it would be £400); in addition to this their two children are both supported by the husband; this costs him about £75 per annum, so that his income is only £125.

It would be difficult to find a better example of the urgent need for a revision of our working social concepts than is afforded by the purely formal notion of "sex equality." Like other ideas deriving from the unreal thought-world of eighteenth-century rationalism mixed with Rousseauistic sentimental optimism, it leads, in practice, to results diametrically opposite to those envisaged by its original promoters. Just as the rationalistic doctrine of "equality" in social life has led to economic inequalities far greater than those which existed in the mediaeval world, before the era of French Revolutionary doctrinairism, so this sister doctrine of "sex equality" (although only partially applied in this country) has already given us social conditions which clearly tend to raise one sex above the other.

In both cases it is the disastrous divorce between doctrine and reality that has led us into the morass. No solution of the sex-equality problem is of any value that does not face fully and frankly all the economical, biological, and psychological *real factors* in the complex relationships of the sexes. The sterile rational doctrinairism of the J. S. Mill–Olive Schreiner–Buss and Beale school was never anything but a pen-and-ink presentation of the problem.

CHAPTER IX

THE PSYCHOLOGY OF SEX

a. MAN AND WOMAN
b. WOMAN AND THE RACE
c. SOME RECENT CONTRIBUTIONS TO SEX PSYCHOLOGY

a. MAN AND WOMAN

A very favourite objection to sex psychology, in so far as it deals with typical sex differences between men and women, runs on these lines, "Oh, but it is impossible to say that men (or women, as the case may be) have such and such attributes, because they are individuals rather than members of a sex; the differences in intellect between Smith and Jones, both men, are often greater by far than any differences of this kind which it is suggested exist between men in general and women in general."

Perhaps this attitude is best understood as a demonstration of the modern dislike of general statements referred to in Chap. II. In reality, one might as well say that there were no characteristics common to trees, because fir-trees and oaks are so different. No one could be so foolish as to deny the enormous differences between different men, or to suggest that these are not far greater than the quantitative differences between a typical man and a typical woman. These arguments have, in reality, nothing to do with comparative sex psychology. Mrs. A. may be ten times more intellectual than the gardener she employs; but when it is a question of the capacity to regard a problem from an abstract standpoint, untinged by emotion, the gardener will probably show that he is a man and Mrs. A. is a woman, despite all the difference in intellectual capacity. To suggest that men are, for example, more intellectual than women is foolish; but to say that there is a special brand of male intellectuality differing in *quality* from the female is a sound statement. No one with any knowledge of life and human psychology would deny (to take an example) that it is an exceedingly rare thing to find in even the ablest man that exact kind of intuition which marks a very average woman. On the other hand, masculine objectivity of mind is hardly ever—perhaps never—found in women.

We are dealing here not with degrees of the same things but with different things. A woman is a woman through and through, so that everything she does is done in a *different* way. As D. H. Lawrence said, the entire polarity of woman is other than that of man, so that all her thoughts and actions are tinged with emotions of which a man knows nothing.

This word of preliminary explanation is necessary in order to remove the possible notion that sex psychology proceeds along the crude "men are this" and "women are that" lines.

It must be emphasised that there is not, and cannot be, such a thing as a clear-cut scheme. It is impossible to put all men or all women into any one category. Just as the colour yellow in the solar spectrum merges imperceptibly into red, so the qualities of the one sex merge into those of the other. Nevertheless, just as there *is* a colour yellow and a colour red, even when they cannot easily be separated, there is a normal masculine psychology and there is a normal feminine psychology, in spite of a large army of exceptions, and of individuals whose characteristics are vague.[1]

There exists a large body of evidence, accumulated by strictly objective methods and by investigators of a dozen nationalities working independently of one another, all tending to show that certain definite mental and emotional characteristics, and groups of characteristics, are associated with sex. The last ten years or so has seen a great increase in the amount and weight of this evidence.

. . . . .

This is not a treatise on physiology, and it is not proposed to take up in any detail the physical differences between the sexes; but by way of approach to the psychological differences it will be useful to mention, in passing, a few points of special significance.

The normal woman of western civilisation is smaller and lighter (by some 15 to 20 lb.) than the normal man; the muscles are not only absolutely less in weight than those of the man but also relatively (i.e. the percentage

[1] A great deal of mystification and confusion has been brought into the question of sex distinction by those who say: "There is a feminine element in every man and a masculine element in every woman; these are so blended that there can be no such thing as a definite psychology of sex." But normally the male in the female is recessive, and vice versa. If it ceases to be recessive, abnormal and dangerous psychological conditions may result. For this very reason it is specially important, in the work of education, to keep a clear grip of sex distinction, although in many individual cases they may be a background of elements more proper to the other sex. As Dr. C. G. Jung says: "A man can live the feminine in himself, and a woman the masculine in herself. None the less, in man the feminine is in the background, as is the masculine in woman. If one lives out the opposite sex in oneself, one is living in one's own background, and that restricts too much the essential individuality. A man should live as a man, and a woman as a woman." (*The New Adelphi*, September 1928.)

of the total weight taken up by the muscles is smaller in the woman than in the man). There are, too, important differences in the constitution and circulation of the blood, and in the nature and functioning of the ductless glands; and both of these factors are necessarily of great significance with respect to both physique and mentality.

The average height of the North European man is about 5 feet 7 inches; of the woman, 5 feet 3 inches. Recent experiments show that the physical strength of young men is related to that of young women in the ratio of 100 to between 70 and 80 (it is of some importance to note that this ratio also holds good amongst savages).

Recent years have seen a most remarkable development in our knowledge of the complicated system of the ductless glands and their secretions (endocrinology); and there can be no doubt that this system plays a much larger part than had hitherto been known in determining the growth and also the mental and emotional characteristics of the organism. The study of these secretions forms one of the most important chapters in modern physiological-psychology, and it is clear that they have much to do with the determination of physical and mental sex differences. It is perhaps in respect of the ductless glands, more than in any other field, that we see how inextricably the psychic and the physical are interrelated—the slightest defect in the functioning of these glands may produce mental and emotional changes that are quite startling.

The differences in the structure of the nervous system, as between men and women, are of particular importance in their connection with education and occupation. This complicated subject cannot be taken up here, but it may be remarked, in passing, that in the normal woman the sympathetic nervous system (which in the female is connected with important internal organs non-existent in the male) plays a larger part than with the man—an observation which fits in with the general conception of woman's psychology unfolded in this chapter.[1]

. . . . .

If we continually bear in mind the different rôles which the sexes have played down the great perspective of human history, we shall not fail to secure the proper point of view for our purpose. Each sex has its own biological

[1] A popular, and yet thoroughly scientific, brief account of sex differences is *Sex*, by Professors Patrick Geddes and J. A. Thomson, from which I take the following extracts:

"While there are undoubtedly differences between man and woman which are modificational or nurtural—the individual results of disparities or peculiarities in their education, training, and occupations—many of the differences are constitutional; inborn, not made. They are intrinsic, not tacked on; of ancient origin, and therefore not liable to change quickly. They have a deep naturalness, and attempts to minimise them are not likely to spell progress. . . . As Havelock Ellis says: 'A man is a man to his very thumbs, and a woman is a woman down to her little toes.' . . . The differences are correlated, they hang together, they are outcrops of the deep fundamental distinction. We may say that the tenacity of life, the longer life, the characteristic endurance, the greater resistance to disease, the smaller percentage of genius, insanity, idiocy, suicide, and crime, and so on, are all correlated with the distinctively female constitution, which may be theoretically regarded as relatively more constructive in its protoplasmic metabolism." Paraphrasing this statement, one may say that the female organism has been admirably adapted by Nature for her racial task of maternity, which demands an immense metabolic effort; while man, with his tendency to externalise his energy, has been fitted for the work of the world. "Man is more given to experiment both with his body and his mind and with other people; man uses more oxygen and combustible material and has more waste in consequence; man's blood has a higher specific gravity, more red blood corpuscles, more haemoglobin; man is the relatively more active type."

history, and this is stamped in the present make-up of each. It would be as impossible to alter, at this time of day, the qualities which man and woman have acquired as the result of millions of years of development as it would be to alter any other product of evolution, such as the habit of going on two legs. As Huxley said: "What has been decided amongst prehistoric protozoa cannot be cancelled by Parliament."

In the course of evolution the male of the species has had occasion to develop his cerebro-spinal nervous system more than the female has developed hers, since her functions have been such as to develop the sympathetic nervous system more especially. In accordance with this biological history, the female is normally swifter and more sensitive in her reactions to emotions (such as joy, fear, grief, or hope). Her greater sensibility, while a valuable quality, tends to make her unstable and subjective. It is a truism to say that women are more influenced by their feelings (say, in their judgment of individuals) than are men. All these qualities follow from the general structure of the female organism. If women possessed a nervous system identical with that of the male, they would be totally unfitted for their maternal functions. Paradoxically, women, although more emotional (and less sentimental) than men, are able, as is well known, to bear pain much better, and possess in general a superior capacity of resisting suffering and illness (hence the notorious higher mortality of boy-babies). This, again, is part of Nature's scheme. It has often been truly said that if men had to bear the children of the race, we should soon be hastening towards extinction. The remarkable vitality and passive endurance of women is needful for the survival of the race. The paradox by which women are outwardly more sensitive than men, while really possessing more endurance, is explained by the greater elasticity and adaptability of the female nervous system. When confronted with some danger, such as a fire or a violent storm, women as a rule show the outward signs of fear or disturbance much sooner than men—in a street panic women nearly always faint in greater numbers than men. All this is natural when we consider the peculiar structure of the female organism. Yet, when put to the point of enduring any trial of vital force, women will generally come through better than men, which is explained by their inherited capacity for passive endurance.

The above may be placed in another light by saying that, broadly speaking, the subconscious and instinctive aspects of human personality are stronger in women, while the conscious and rational side is much more developed in men. Outwardly, the man, whose reactions are more controlled than the woman's, shows less sign of fear or disturbance; but owing to his inferior instinctive power he finds it more difficult to survive, for example, an exhausting operation than would a woman. As a doctor has expressed it: the woman faces the operation showing every sign of perturbation and alarm, but survives; the man clenches his teeth, shows no outward signs of fear, and—dies!

If women have more passive endurance, men have more initiative. The chief strength of the male lies in his superior originality and initiative. And both of these qualities are corollaries of the masculine power of detachment—of man's ability to stand outside and above his work and functions as well as within them.

b. WOMAN AND THE RACE

To quote Dr. Arabella Kenealy, woman "remains at core a creature of instinct, not of reason. As a creature of instinct she is invaluable to Life—because Life is moulded upon instinct." The intellectual work of woman unfolds itself within a framework built by man, just as the physical life of man develops within a framework built by woman.

It is as *the custodian of life*—using the phrase in its very widest sense—that woman makes her unique contribution to civilisation.

It has been well said that man is for the race, but woman *is* the race. The masculine characteristics are those useful for the work of the world—practical energy, reasoning power, scientific sense, initiative, will-power; the feminine characteristics are those necessary for the preservation of the race—maternal instinct, selfless devotion, patience, cheerful endurance, adaptability to circumstances, sympathy, intuition.

Mr. A. M. Ludovici hits the nail square on the head when he says (in *Woman: A Vindication*) that woman's chief attributes are those which "make for a continuance of the human species on earth," and as being "of so much moment . . . that they overshadow every catalogue of foibles or vices that has ever been drawn up against her by a Weininger or a Schopenhauer."

From this point of view many seemingly enigmatical things become clear and obvious. The popular idea that women are cowardly and weak as compared with men is at once refuted by the fact that women will show incredible courage on behalf of anyone to whom they are attached. As a matter of fact, there is some truth both in the popular idea and in its refutation. The preservation of the species requires from woman, on the one hand, that she should be cautious and fearful to a degree, in order that she may be constantly on the look-out for danger threatening her beloved offspring or mate; and on the other, that she should be as bold as a female tiger in defence of, or devotion to, man or child; and woman, being far nearer to Nature than man, responds with ease to demands apparently so incompatible. The pages of history and the experience of our daily lives abound with examples of women who have displayed, when it was called for, a truly astounding courage and stoicism (such as that exhibited by the heroic women of the Indian Mutiny days), and yet who were, in their daily life, ultra-feminine in the early-Victorian sense of the term—that is, nervous, sensitive, emotional, and easily liable to tears. (Cf. also the heroines in Shakespeare's plays.)

It is, in fact, precisely this plasticity of character, this ready transition from one state of mind to another according to the demands of the moment, which is so typical of the normal woman. It is part of the adaptability which Nature has developed in the female for racial purposes. The firm, rational, strong-willed, independent type of woman who is no rarity to-day is, in reality, a departure from the normal feminine. She is the product of a highly artificial system of life and education, and will, in all probability, by reason of sterility, prove to be an evolutionary reject.

. . . . .

One of the many evil results of modern pseudo-equalitarian doctrines is that public opinion is thereby led to value and judge women by the prevailing (i.e. masculine) standards, with the result that woman's real character is completely misunderstood. Seen in its true light, as racially needful and as essentially complementary (and not similar) to man's character, it acquires at once *a higher position and a truer understanding*. At present woman suffers heavily from the circumstance that she is expected to justify herself according to standards that are not her own.

In her essence, woman is the incarnation of "the will-to-live." Primarily concerned with the creation and nurture of life itself in the flesh, it would be strange indeed if she could stop to elaborate the abstract rules and norms which seem to men so important; and for this reason woman often acts in what, to the male, seems a wilful and irresponsible fashion, although perhaps in this very moment she is most of all obeying the will of her mistress, Nature.

> The man's a fool who tries by force or skill
> To stem the current of a woman's will;
> For if she will, she will, you may depend on't,
> And if she won't, she won't, and there's an end on't.

We must avoid making generalisations which, taken too literally, will seem crude, but we should not be far from the mark in saying that woman's mentality centres in *the concrete and actual*, either outward or inward; while the masculine mentality, in its typical form, has its roots in the world of the abstract and rational.[1] Women are

[1] Dr. Oskar Schultze, one of the most scientific investigators in this field, is of the opinion that all students of sex psychology must agree in attributing to women a superiority over men in the emotional perception of the concrete and individual. He regards these characteristics as being bound up with woman's physical constitution, and especially with the important rôle played by the sympathetic nervous system. "The womanly lack of sense for the abstract cannot be much

extraordinarily aware of reality in its immediacy, whether this be given in the form of an external object, such as another person, or makes itself felt as a feeling, such as fear, hate, or love.

A vast amount of friction between the sexes is due to the fact that men rely upon *reason*, while women are actuated by motives drawn from the *subconscious*. It thus appears to the man that the woman is unreasonable, whimsical, and erratic, and he becomes impatient at her imperviousness to his rational arguments. On the other hand, the woman finds male reason pedantic, absurd, and unreal. The remedy for such friction is better understanding between the sexes, but this can be brought about only through true psychological insight, and not through the education of women along masculine lines. With such insight each sex should learn to respect and value the specific attributes of the other. One of the worst results of the current levelling-down of distinctions in this sphere is that this healthy mutual respect is undermined.

In its place we get the cult of an unnatural pseudo-equality, which, so far from bringing the sexes nearer together, forces them apart. For the attraction of the sexes for one another is the age-long need of woman by man, and of man by woman, the search for the self-complementary opposite, for the personality who will fulfil the lack in self. Taking up this standpoint, it is

altered by education or instruction, because it is rooted in woman's physiological structure." Women, it is added, have a stronger memory than men for all those ideas, recollections, and experiences that are tinged with emotion; they participate more warmly in the inner life of the individual, and possess a better intuitive knowledge of human nature, as well as more altruism and more capacity for sympathy, patience, and self-abnegation. (*Das Weib*, by Oskar Schultze and Max Hirsch, Leipzig, Curt Kabitsch, 1928.)

easy enough to understand the curious atmosphere of sex antipathy which is so noticeable in the Anglo-Saxon lands.[1] For when the mentality of either man or woman begins to be dominated by a purely abstract doctrine of sex equality, at once trouble creeps in. Every little difference in position or privilege, real or apparent, immediately becomes a ground for envy or resentment, instead of appearing as part of the natural order of things.

c. SOME RECENT CONTRIBUTIONS TO SEX PSYCHOLOGY

In reviewing the literature of sex psychology, we cannot fail to be impressed by the *unanimity* which exists between writers of different nationalities and different schools of thought. For example, Professor Heymans shows us that a report on the characteristics and abilities of French women students, prepared by a number of French professors and teachers, gave results which, from a psychological point of view, were almost identical with those obtained from a similar report prepared (wholly independently) in Germany by German professors and teachers. The Englishman, Havelock Ellis; the American, Stanley Hall; the Dutchman, Heymans; the Germans, Schultze, Lippmann, and Heilbronn; and the Swiss, Klages (to mention only one or two leading names), all come to conclusions which, if not identical, are so similar as to make quite absurd the view that there is no such thing as well-established knowledge on the subject of sex distinction.

The broad outlines of typical sex distinction have been

[1] Cf. H. G. Wells, *The World of William Clissold*, vi, i: "I cannot help but recognise the atmosphere of intensifying sex antagonism in which we are living."

indicated in the foregoing sections. This typical distinction is corroborated not only by modern observation but by the opinions expressed throughout history by men and women of all nations, from East to West, and North to South. It is supported by our proverbs and saws, by the visions of poets, and by the literary analysis of our novelists. In modern times it has been expressed with poetic insight by Shakespeare and Goethe, perhaps the two ripest minds of modern Europe.

. . . . .

In one of the most modern works on sex psychology, that of Professor Heymans, of Groningen (Holland)—obtainable in an excellent German translation entitled *Die Psychologie der Frauen*—we have an analysis of masculine and feminine characteristics which is of great value for all who wish to study seriously the problems touched upon in this chapter—an analysis based not upon mere opinion or theory but almost wholly upon an immense series of exact observations carried out mainly upon students and boys and girls, but also, to some extent, upon older persons.

Professor Heymans sent out inquiry papers to fifty-four Dutch schools, containing questions as to character and ability, with special reference to sex. All these papers were filled up quite independently; and yet, in almost every respect, the hundreds of teachers who filled in the answers agree in their estimates of male and female ability. Similar inquiries were conducted, through the medium of trained scientific observers, as to the distinctive mental and emotional characteristics of persons known very closely to them (in all some 2,500 in number). A comparison of the results obtained by this last method agreed closely with the result obtained from the schools, although there was no relationship between the two investigations. It would be inconceivable that such a degree of correspondence could be due to coincidence. Professor Heymans also brings in the results of the above-mentioned French and German analyses, and the results of a very careful investigation of the abilities and characteristics of Dutch students at *all* the Dutch universities. For details the reader is referred to the book itself.

In a table summing up the observations upon students (in particular) we find that the men easily led in the application of knowledge, in originality of thought, depth of special knowledge, love of independent reading (i.e. in reading apart from examination purposes), powers of logic, and abstract thought in general; in critical capacity, in initiative, in love of science, and (rather unexpectedly) in practical dexterity (in experimental work, and so forth). Those qualities in which the girl students exhibited a clearly marked superiority were mainly of a moral order, such as perseverance, application to studies, order, good attendance, patience, conscientiousness, and general "steadiness." In memory and in school knowledge they were also placed above the men, and in "keenness." In some directions, such as originality and power of abstract thought, their inferiority was very marked indeed.

It would appear, according to Professor Heymans, that (making a very broad distinction) it is the abstract which appeals to the male and the concrete to the female (in the abstract we include technics); and he quotes Havelock Ellis: "The masculine preference is for the more remote, the constructive, the useful, the general, and the abstract"; the feminine preference for "the finished product, the ornamental, the individual, and the concrete." "The bloodless coldness of abstraction is inwardly repugnant to women, because their emotional needs find no satisfaction in this field," writes Heymans. Further, he quotes from the philosopher Lotze: "The knowledge and will of the man is taken up with the general, that of the woman with the complete whole. . . . Women hate analysis, while they enjoy and admire the finished whole, in its completeness, in its immediate value and beauty."

As an example of the feminine indifference to analysis we may note the extreme rarity of the little girl who takes her toys to pieces to see how they work, a form of activity which is one of the most typical characteristics of small boys. The girl loves to arrange her toys and to have a personal relationship with them, but she is not at all interested in knowing how they work.

. . . . .

One of the most interesting attempts to set forth salient mental sex distinctions we owe to Ludwig Klages, of Zurich, whose works on character-psychology have aroused great interest. He has for many years made human character, its types and distinctions, his special study, and his opinion on the subject of this chapter is of considerable weight. Amongst masculine qualities he places in the front rank: objectivity and the power of abstraction, the capacity of absorption in impersonal matters (as the drawback to this quality, men are much less realistic than women and more likely to be the victims of illusion). Practical energy and initiative, too, are more frequently found in the male, but these qualities often degenerate into lack of feeling and restlessness.

In width of vision, imagination, and many-sidedness, men are also given first place. In general, Klages regards the male psychology as being marked by strong differentiation and a lack of inner unity. The man can more easily split up his personality. The woman, on the other hand, is much more a unity. Whatever she does she does with wholeness, and the oneness of her nature makes it much more difficult for her to detach herself from subjective impulses. Women are more closely bound up with nature and all that is elementary, and less liable to self-deception (the drawback to these qualities being the dependence of women upon the personal side of life and their lack of objectivity). Klages lays weight on woman's sense of concrete reality and comparative immunity from illusion, and on her intuitive faculty (accompanied often by opacity to reason). Woman's patience, devotion, and strong sense of pity, and her natural warmth of feeling, are amongst the other points in Klages's list of feminine attributes.

For our study it is of significance that one who has approached the whole problem of sex distinction from a fresh standpoint, quite uninfluenced by what others may have said, relying wholly on his own personal observations, should have thus reaffirmed the broad lines of distinction which have been placed before the reader of this chapter.

CHAPTER X

THE GIRL AND HER EDUCATION

a. PSEUDO-MASCULINISM

It is necessary to go back more than fifty years in order to understand the present position with regard to the education of girls.

We are still under the influence of a quite one-sided and unthinking reaction against the extreme narrowness of the Victorian outlook. Just because eighty years ago girls were brought up along "womanly" lines, it is now taken for granted, without any further examination of the rights and wrongs of the matter, that their education must take no notice whatever of sex. One of the most urgent needs of the day is to get right away from both these prejudices and to examine the problem from a detached scientific standpoint.

Is it really true that girls should be brought up without any reference to their distinctive psychology? The moment this plain question is asked the absurdity of the modern educational ideal becomes apparent.

It was, no doubt, necessary to break down the narrow Victorian outlook, and the pioneers of women's emancipation did a good work in showing that girls can equal boys.

But now that we are in possession of a wealth of

knowledge as to the deep differences between the sexes in mind, body, and nervous constitution, the retention of this imitative attitude on the part of girls' schools is out-of-date and demonstrably contrary to the interests of their pupils.

Fortunately a reaction is now setting in, led largely by thoughtful women.

Thus Mrs. Florence Low—a very competent authority—writes: "To-day the curriculum and the examinations in the girls' schools are practically the same as boys . . . this absolute similarity is injurious to women and harmful to the nation. It has helped to change the girl's outlook and attitude towards life, and to give her the boy's ideals and aims . . . our modern education of girls is, I think, the greatest compliment ever paid to men by our sex!" Many women teachers, she continues, "desire a time-table with a more feminine bias, an education in which the peculiarly feminine qualities will have more chance of development and the pupils will be more specifically prepared for their *métier de femme.*" (From an article in *Britannia*, January 4, 1929.)

Miss Cowdray (head of the Crouch End Girls' High School), amongst other experienced women teachers, has recently protested most emphatically against the one-sided orientation of the education of women in England, with its almost total neglect of the biological and racial aspects of life.

It is every day becoming clearer that women cannot be permanently satisfied with modes of life which pay no attention to their specific psychology, and fail to fit them for their most interesting and vital life-tasks. Thus Mrs. Dora Russell, after pointing out the failure of the early feminists to appreciate the significance of sex distinction, writes: "There never has been a period when education has trained women for the possibility of motherhood, and it is time that such training was begun. ... To me, the important task of modern feminism is to accept and proclaim sex. . . ." (*Hypatia*, chap. ii.) Mrs. Haldane, in her admirable little book, *Motherhood and its Enemies*, reveals a similar realisation of the inadequacy of modern educational methods in view of woman's racial task. Mothers, she insists, are not simply born; it is folly to think that girls who have been trained solely with a view to economic independence will, by some miracle, become fitted by the mere act of marriage to discharge functions for which their previous life has left them entirely unprepared.

The great boys' schools, despite their defects, embody a long tradition, an immense experience of boyish ways and needs. The girls' school of to-day, on the other hand, is a new-fangled creation evolved for the most part under the influence of the unpsychological ideals of pre-war days, when to prove that girls were not inferior to boys was the one aim that counted. It is in no way based upon a study of *the actual psychological and biological needs of girls*.[1]

[1] From the Blue Book, *Differentiation of Curricula between the Sexes in Secondary Schools* (section on the History of Girls' Schools), I take the following passage:

"Basing their policy on the belief that girls could equal boys, at least in intellectual matters, if favourable conditions were afforded, the leaders of the [women's] movement implicitly assumed that what had been done for and by boys was in general suitable for both sexes." During the critical period, 1850–70, when the foundations of girls' education in England were laid, it is perfectly clear (as we see in this Blue Book) that the imitation of male education was the all-important matter. On p. 33 we read: "A fresh phase in the process of assimilating the girls' curriculum to that for boys was marked by the rise of the more modern boarding-schools for girls [such as St. Leonard's and

When the old Norman fisherwoman in Mr. Mottram's novel, *The English Miss*, saw the heroine bounding down the slope to the sea, she cried out, *Ça c'est une anglaise!* Her slim, athletic, boyish appearance proclaimed Marny to be a daughter of Albion. Her enthusiasm for boyish games, her scorn of womanhood, her determination never to admit, even to herself, that she is not a boy—all these things are characteristic, implies the author, of the modern English girl. Nowhere else, save possibly in certain American circles, do we find the same passionate repudiation of their biological life-rôle amongst the young females of the species.

It is time that we asked ourselves: What does it all mean? Why this headlong flight from the inescapable? this "blind revolt against reality," in the phrase of Dr. Adler.[1]

. . . . .

Modern psychology is apparently a sealed book to those responsible for the education of girls in England. There is no indication that they have profited in the least from the immensely important advances in psychological knowledge due to such men as Dr. Havelock Ellis, Dr. Stanley Hall, and the pioneers of the psycho-analytical school. They are still almost wholly under the

Roedean] which reproduced in almost all respects the arrangements in vogue at boys' public schools. . . . The ideals fostered in these schools are being widely spread by mistresses and old pupils who are now teaching in High Schools and County Municipal Schools."

[1] The most probable explanation is that put forward by Dr. Adler in his recent work, *The Science of Living*: The standards of modern life are such as to discredit the specifically feminine; this has given woman a strong feeling of inferiority, which she seeks to compensate through a violent effort to achieve masculine aims and standards.

influence of the notion that the teacher's function is to rectify the error of Nature in having created two sexes!

The motto of Olive Schreiner, "We claim all labour for our province!" necessary as it was at that time, when women were escaping from the narrowness of Victorianism, has now come to stand for a type of sexless education which flies in the face of modern sex psychology and starves the emotional life of our girls.

The entire system of ideas which lies behind the present-day education of girls is more than forty years out-of-date. It derives from the unpsychological and unbiological life-outlook of the John Stuart Mill school, continued in the utilitarian pseudo-masculine feminism of Olive Schreiner, and applied to education by such women as Miss Buss, Miss Beale, and Miss Emily Davies.

This whole tendency is dominated by the "dead-level" view of sex equality, the belief that women can prove their worth only by becoming in all respects identical with men. The modern view of sex equality, based upon the equal valuation of different functions, has yet to make itself felt in the educational world, although it is already supreme in the field of ideas.[1] No present-day

[1] One of the profoundest and most sensitive studies of the sex-equality question to be found in modern literature is the article "Die Wertfrage zwischen den Geschlechtern" (*Zeitschrift für Menschenkunde*, May 1926), by the well-known German writer on psychology and social subjects, Oskar A. H. Schmitz, who takes up the standpoint that the polarity of man and woman is a metaphysical principle essential to the stability of all human society, and containing in itself the idea of equality, since neither is, in an ultimate sense, independent of the other. "The human race would not have appeared upon earth in two sexes, unless each of the two forms had to express a meaning of its own. People may deny this differentiation of sex, since it is not possible to reduce it to a formula, but reality will not be mocked. . . . The confusion which to-day reigns in respect of sex equality has been brought about by those who no longer feel quite sure that they really

thinker of repute would venture to take his stand upon the sexless psychology of Mill and his followers.

b. THE FLIGHT FROM SEX

Every educational system is the product of a certain life-outlook. Behind the present-day education of girls lies the idea that women are not really necessary. It is evidently believed that men represent all that is worth while in life. Hence women can do nothing better than imitate them. Quite forgotten is the ancient truth—at one time accepted as a truism—that society needs for its existence two modes of being, the male and the female, each with its own appropriate psychology. To-day, the mere suggestion that girls should be "womanly" would be received with shrieks of laughter. The idea that there is another pole to life, that everything does not rotate about the masculine axis, is being denied (subconsciously if not consciously) in most of our modern girls' schools and colleges.

are equal; in other words, by women who are no longer fully self-confident as *women*, but who have fallen under the spell of masculine suggestion, and are painfully anxious to demonstrate that women are just as capable as men of producing achievements of the masculine type because they are firmly convinced in their own minds that what is womanly can never be as valuable as that which is manly. . . . It is essential that, transcending the conflict, we should seek to win a new insight into the meaning of the two forms of humanity, man and woman; not with the reactionary purpose of depriving women of any of their painfully won rights, but in the hope that women will, through a realisation of their nature (and many have already attained to this standpoint), again desire of their own free will to be women, although the possibility of following the opposite path is open to them. . . . The problem of equality becomes hopelessly muddled if we measure women against men, instead of by their own standards." In a work entitled *Wespennester* (vol. i, part ii), Schmitz has recently still further developed his ideas.

For this astonishing state of things there are many causes: for example, the triumph of industrialism, the rationalisation of all our values, the decline of home-life, and the decay of religion.

If anyone should doubt that the whole female side of life has fallen into utter contempt, let him follow my example and make a study of current utterances with regard to girls and their education. During the last three or four years I have read some hundreds of review and newspaper articles upon these subjects, and in practically all of these the following adjectives were made use of to describe the girl of to-day: sensible, level-headed, sane, healthy, candid, frank, independent, truthful, and efficient. Very useful qualities, no doubt. But where are the *feminine* qualities? In not one of these articles did such terms as maternal, intuitive, adaptable, tender, or gracious occur at all (just to pick out one or two qualities that have more usually been associated with the female sex).

In 1868, George Eliot wrote to Miss Davies, then busy with the creation of Girton College, and warned her of the danger of forgetting that the natural distinction of sex (in mind as well as body) is essential to all deeper human culture. The warning has proved to be even more necessary than the great novelist could have dreamed.

A thousand pities that the Women's Movement did not listen to the humanity and wisdom of Marian Evans the *woman*, rather than to the thin and bloodless theories of the male doctrinaire Mill!

. . . . .

Of course it will at once be said: "Yes, but the girl of to-day must go out into the world and become independent because she cannot reckon on marriage." Now there would be something in this argument (although, as a matter of fact, there is no real numerical excess of marriageable women over men, see p. 169) if those who used it regarded the entry of women into male careers as an *evil*, and were apologising for its necessity. But this is not their position at all. Quite the contrary. They are fully convinced of the *essential inferiority* of the feminine side of life.

The girl working in a factory regards herself as a very superior person indeed as compared with the girl who goes out as nursemaid. But is it true that looking after machines is a nobler or better task than looking after growing human beings, and watching the ever-fresh process of their mental unfoldment? What a monstrous perversion of moral values lies behind our modern outlook in these matters. We must ask ourselves: "How have we managed to stray so far from the path of common sense and sound racial instincts?"

It is clear that what we are witnessing to-day is the collapse of feminism (in the only true sense of the term) and the victory of the man-made mechanical life-outlook over the soul of woman herself. The world of business, machinery, "efficiency," science, and, in short, of all that is impersonal and hostile to woman's natural genius, has triumphed terribly over the world of the eternal feminine—personal life, home, sex, children, nature, and life-creation.[1] Girls' schools, following the lead of Olive

[1] Quite typical of the popular cult of pseudo-masculinism is an article by Rosita Forbes which appeared in *Nash's Magazine* (September 1931). I quote one or two passages: "Personal relationships are very agreeable if you don't turn them into responsibilities. They are relaxations, just like any other amusement or occupation. . . . Fifty years ago men and women devoted themselves to each other. . . . The

Schreiner, have become feeding-pipes for the machine of industry, and have long ceased even to consider education from the standpoint of human values. Small wonder, then, that they now turn out, by tens of thousands, young women whose hearts are filled with revolt and bitterness, even if they are, as a rule, so totally unaware of their real plight as often to imagine that enlarged opportunities within the machine are all that they need!

What was originally envisaged as the preparation of girls for eventual non-marriage has now become a vast machinery for automatically destroying the marriage opportunities of young women. It is now known that the main factor in making marriage difficult and improbable is not (as was formerly supposed) the excess in numbers of young women over young men (now trifling), but the economic situation created by the immense influx of girls into the labour market, which enormously diminishes the possibilities of marriage for young men and correspondingly for their girl friends. As a resultant

world was obsessed by this need of domestic sacrifice. . . . To-day we are all apt to ask 'Why should we? What good is it going to do?' Life is harder and crueller and infinitely more busy than it used to be. We've so much to do that we cut out everything that isn't essential—for ordinary people to-day the main problem of life is not the much advertised one of how to keep the affections of a husband or a wife or anyone else, but *how to keep themselves*."

Here we see, clearly enough, the modern idea that only the impersonal counts; that love is not a reality; and that the ideal life is that of ego-centricity. Very interesting in this (as in all other utterances of the type) is the utter passivity of mood—life is getting harder and more cruel, and the only thing to do is to drift with this tendency and make it more hard and more cruel! As was suggested in Chapter II of this study, behind the façade of freedom-loving individualism lies *complete capitulation to the mechanistic life-philosophy*.

(This note should also be read in connection with p. 201.)

of this state of things innumerable girls desirous of marriage and home-life are now engaged in displacing the very men who might, were things otherwise organised, have been their husbands.[1]

c. THE HEALTH QUESTION

As a consequence of the "lag" which separates our actual working practice in the education of girls from our theoretical knowledge, we find that all over the country countless thousands of young girls are being forced through examinations and encouraged in the playing of all sorts of strenuous games and sports at an age when, in the opinion of competent medical men and psychologists, it is essential that they should refrain from all severe mental and physical strain.

There is every reason to believe, with Dr. Arabella Kenealy, that the efficiency of the modern girl in all sorts of masculine occupations and sports has been paid for with a high price. Nature has built up the physique and nervous system of woman with a view, primarily, to her racial functions, which require a large potential energy; and when girls are unduly "forced," or when they

[1] An amazing amount of ignorance still prevails as to the true numerical proportions of the sexes—many educated people are firmly convinced that there are at least two women to every man. There are, it is true, some 1½ million more women than men, but this is not a large excess in a population of nearly fifty million; and, moreover, this excess is chiefly in the *older* section of the population. In 1926, there were 5,180,000 females between 15 and 30; and 4,880,000 males. If we regard the marriageable ages for women as being 20 to 45, and for men 20 to 50, we arrive at the surprising result that there were actually 8 million possible husbands for 7·9 million young women!

develop a masculine robustness of muscle (unnecessary for women), much of the nervous force which should remain stored up for future racial uses is either used up or deflected into other channels. In her work, *Feminism and Sex Extinction*, we read:

"Just at the age when Nature locks the door upon her constitutional resources for the purpose of evolving these to higher organisation, the schools and industries do a strenuous best to keep the door forcibly open, and to wrest the resources from the storehouse of potential . . . the natural languors and disabilities of the girl's adolescent phase are vigorously combated."

In consequence of this mistaken type of education, the finer and softer attributes of womanhood, which are as indispensable to the race as they are superfluous to the machine of industry, often fail of fruition. We get "Amazons of the hockey, football, tennis, or hunting fields, only just distinguishable in general characteristics from the male"; and later in life these types often pay severely for their unnatural development. Dr. Kenealy points out (p. 120) that when adolescent girls are "strained by athletics, by over-culture, or industrial exhaustion, the vital resources are so diverted from the evolution of function as to cause incapacitation in them, partial or complete, for wifehood, and for the bearing of sound and fine offspring." On p. 135 she quotes a well-known American gynaecologist, Dr. Gaillard Thomas, who estimated, some years ago, that "only about 4 per cent of American women proper were physiologically fitted to become wives and mothers." Professor Stanley Hall also published a large mass of statistics (see *Adolescence*) showing the positively alarming unfitness of the Anglo-Saxon woman for maternity; and he attributed this very serious state of things largely to the failure of present-day educators to pay sufficient attention to the vital difference of the sexes. Another well-known authority, the late Professor G. J. Engelmann, who possessed an exceptionally wide experience in America, wrote: "It appears to be a fact that women who develop their muscular system highly suffer exceptionally in child-birth." (Quoted from *Weib und Mann*, translated as "The Opposite Sexes," by Dr. Heilbronn.)[1]

Dr. Olive Wheeler, Professor of Education at University College, Cardiff, and one of the leading authorities on the education of girls, admits candidly, in her work *Youth*, that the present higher education system is highly injurious to the health of girls; on p. 31 she quotes figures showing that of 2,000 London secondary schoolgirls about 8 per cent suffered from anaemia, 17 per cent from spinal curvature, and 7 per cent from flat feet, and these defects showed a tendency to increase during early adolescence: "In the case of boys there is an increased liability to certain kinds of lung and heart trouble,

[1] Speaking of schools for upper and middle-class children, the well-known authority on hygiene, Dr. Leonard Williams, says (*Daily Mail*, December 27, 1930) the tendency is "towards a rather unbridled furtherance of intensive muscular exertion of a combative and competitive kind . . . one physical result of such sports is heart trouble in later life, but that does not comprise the whole story. Unnatural and unnecessary strains are placed by these sports upon structures and functions which are still in their budding state—with the result that future normal maternity is seriously compromised." Much damage may also be done (he continues) by thus fostering "the male element, which is inherent in every girl," and inhibiting the development of her femininity.

The serious rise in maternal mortality (see my work, *Woman and Society*, p. 46) during the last twenty-five years, despite all medical advances, may very well have much to do with the unsuitable type of education now prevalent.

but the dangers of physical strain do not seem to be nearly so great as with girls.[1]

It would be easy for me to fill many pages with weighty opinions in this sense. The reader is referred to the works of Dr. Havelock Ellis (especially *Sex in Relation to Society*, chap. ii), to Dr. Stanley Hall's standard work, *Adolescence* (vol. ii), and to the Blue Book referred to in the footnote, for a detailed and authoritative treatment of this important matter.

d. THE EGO-CENTRIC LIFE-IDEAL

While it is possible to sympathise with the difficulties of the modern educator or parent, who is more or less compelled to view the education of girls from a practical standpoint—in other words, to train them for a neuter career, this does not in any way abolish the fact that such a training takes no account of the girl's deeper psychology.

[1] The reader is also referred to chap. iv of the Blue Book, *Differentiation of Curricula between the Sexes in Secondary Schools* (H.M.S.O.), from which I take the following passages: "After the onset of adolescence . . . [girls] are on the whole less strong than boys, being more inclined to suffer from nervous strain and more liable to fatigue . . . it seems clear from the evidence that girls need even more careful supervision during adolescence than boys and for a longer period . . . there should be a well-defined difference in the extent of the demands made on boys and girls at school . . . the predisposition of girls to nervous overstrain, especially at the period of adolescence, is one of the most important factors in the problem of female education, necessitating sympathetic differentiation. . . ." The report goes on to say that the question of games and sports in girls' schools should be carefully considered, with a view to further differentiation; the risk of overstrain under existing conditions is "deserving of the most careful attention."

It is noteworthy that the Italian Fascist authorities (who take a most enlightened view of racial questions) have strictly prohibited all competitive athletics for girls; while in France a representative committee of doctors recently petitioned the Government to take similar steps.

We cannot alter the fundamental facts of life. And it will remain true as long as the human race exists that the entire physical and psychological make-up of woman is related to her racial functions. There is here no comparison with the other sex. The characteristics outlined in the foregoing chapter are not merely empirical. They are not simply the qualities that woman *happens* to have, on account of tradition or prejudice. They are those that she *must* have.

It is only possible to deny this by refusing to consider the psychological problem at all. Woman has been fitted by nature for highly specialised functions, and this adjustment also concerns women who have no intention of marriage or parenthood, because it permeates the subconscious as well as the conscious life (in fact, a large part of the disharmony that is so characteristic of many modern women is probably due to the gulf between conscious and subconscious personalities).

Let us assume that it were possible by systematic training along masculine lines, by sport and occupational adjustments, to produce a type of woman identical in all respects, save the purely physical, with the male of the species (this was the sole aim of the old-fashioned type of feminist); what would be the result? Such a woman would be unfitted for mating or maternity. She would be lacking in all the qualities essential to her functions. And the race which had succeeded in producing her would pass into extinction in one generation.

. . . . .

It is a part of that "monstrous perversion of values," to which allusion has been made on p. 167, that when the racial point of view is put forward in connection with the education of girls, it is felt, in some unexplained way, to be derogatory. Yet it is in truth absolutely essential to any psychological view of education.

In *Adolescence* (chap. xvii), Dr. Stanley Hall writes of the girl: "Her whole soul, conscious and unconscious, is best conceived as a magnificent organ of heredity, and to its laws all her psychic activities, if unperverted, are true."

This sentence should be inscribed in large golden letters over the entrance of every girls' school in the land. It contains the very essence of the matter.

Speaking of basic instincts, Dr. Stanford Read says: "We are on safe ground if we divide them mainly into those which are self-preservative and those which are race-preservative. The former may also be termed the ego-instinct, whilst the latter is largely synonymous with the sexual instinct." (*The Struggles of Male Adolescence*, p. 56.)

We might almost define the present-day education of girls as an attempt to develop to the utmost all that portion of the mind of the girl which pivots about the self-preservative instinct, while systematically damming up the flow of interest and power to the centres which make her an "organ of heredity." The examination cramming; the tennis, hockey and other sports; the conversion of interest in the other sex into *camaraderie*; the cult of hardiness, independence, and self-assertion; the inculcation (either deliberately or unconsciously) of a contempt for marriage and home-life—all these things are designed to strengthen the ego-interests and to weaken or destroy the race-interests.

All the same, sex cannot be killed, and when the slumbering and half-murdered instinct does assert itself it is apt to assume crude and uncontrolled forms, and because it finds the ground unprepared, and the sexless ideals which have been formed afford no appropriate points of contact, it may demand an immediately physical fulfilment. The sex instinct has been left naked. An asexual type of education has neglected to develop the thought-forms which might have clothed it with meaning and dignity. Nothing but the crude primitive urge remains. The ideal character-components correlated to the sex impulse, inhibiting and directing it, have not been cultivated. (The reader is referred to the very striking passages on this matter on pp. 329–34 of Keyserling's *America Set Free*.)

What has been said on pp. 85–7 with respect to the plasticity of the libido applies with double force to the girl, in view of the greater impressionability of the feminine nature. The now quite usual view that if we educate girls for careers, giving them an education which, if not definitely masculine, is neuter (suited, that is, to that entirely mythical object, a "human being"), their instinctive nature will look after itself, is in the highest degree unpsychological. In another section (Chapter VI) we have seen what a very vital part is played in development by the form-giving element in education, and how its absence retards growth. In the present-day education of girls there is *no formative principle specifically related to feminine psychology*; and the mere taking over of such principles from masculine education (or from areas of life regarded as "human," i.e. non-sexual) means that large and deeply significant sections of the girl's personality remain without any centre of integration. The result is only too often that division and restlessness which accompanies a disintegrated personality.

A wise education will effect the right balance. But it is precisely my charge against the modern education of girls *that it does not even seek this balance*; its aim, all along, is to prevent the development of the feminine instinctive centres and to deflect the whole of the transferable energy to the self-assertive and sexually neutral areas of the mind. (I do not, of course, suggest that the sex instinct in its direct or physical aspect should be encouraged during school years; the important thing is to encourage the growth of those ideal aspects of the emotional personality which are related to the primitive instinct, and will later on form part of the womanly character-type.)

It is, of course, only too true that there does not exist in English educational circles any desire to produce womanly girls. That is precisely the trouble. But since women were created by nature to be women and not to suffer a process of forcible repression with the object of de-naturalising them, the present methods can only result in causing intense distress.

e. POSITIVE FEMINISM

The conclusions to be derived from the foregoing chapter on the Psychology of Sex may be summarised in a single sentence: Woman has been marvellously equipped, in structure and heredity, for the function of maternity and, in a wider sense, to act as the *custodian of life*.

What importance is attached to this basic fact in the education of girls? None whatever. In a boys' school an attempt (however imperfect) is made to draw out some of the well-known masculine capacities, such as competitive energy, love of science, or social leadership; the teaching is based (at any rate to some extent) upon recognised psychological realities. In a girls' school no one dreams of asking the simple question: What is the psychology of the young girl; and how can we build upon it? To such an extent are these schools dominated by an obsolete doctrinairism alien to reality that it is taken for granted in nine cases out of ten (especially in the big girls' high schools) that there is absolutely nothing in the girl's mind or emotional make-up which distinguishes her in any way from a boy. A couple of years ago I became involved in a controversy with a well-known woman educationist, the head of one of our largest training colleges for women teachers, and this lady wrote me a letter in which she actually asserted that she did not believe in the existence of any ascertainable mental or emotional distinctions between boys and girls or men and women! That the guidance of those about to teach girls should be in the hands of such pillars of obscurantism is sad to contemplate.

The inevitable result of the narrow and essentially *unreal* life-outlook which has imposed itself upon our girls' schools and colleges is that the girl grows up with a large area of her innermost personality violently repressed; and since the avenues of expression which modern feminism has opened up for women are almost exclusively of a wholly sexless nature, this repression of woman's characteristic instinctive life continues into the twenties and thirties. As we have already noted, the marriage opportunities of the modern girl have been reduced enormously, largely by feminism; and it must not be overlooked that the free-love relationships advocated by many feminists (even were they general) are not a substitute for marriage, if only for the reason that they are sterile—not to mention the moral issues involved.

. . . . .

What happens when a girl's whole education revolves around examination work and games, as is now usually the case, is that *the personality as a whole does not attain to maturity*, because a fully-developed young woman is something more than an examination-passing machine or a tennis "fan." In order to secure all-round development the educator must recognise the importance of the feminine life-instincts and supply them with material upon which to feed. The educational ideal must be neither masculine nor neuter (the "human being" ideal), but *positively* feminine.

Suppose that a large girls' high school were to give up some of its cricket or hockey fixtures and to establish in its neighbourhood a nursery school for neglected poor children, and that for one afternoon (or two) every week each of the older classes spent its time caring for and studying these children under competent guidance from a child psychologist, this would be a small advance towards the sort of new orientation which I suggest. Nearly all young girls (before the educational machine grips them) have a profound instinctive attachment to babies. Let this be developed and intensified, and not, as is now the case, deliberately crushed to such an extent that it is hard for it to be reawakened. Such an innovation would be highly popular with the girls and would serve pedagogical ends of much greater importance than the capacity to bowl overhand at cricket or to beat some other school at hockey. This would be a real attempt to take some notice of basic psychological factors, and to persuade the pupils that they are young *women* and not mythical "human beings."

(In elementary schools there are, in a few cases, classes in which instruction in the care of children is given; but what I suggest is something more advanced for girls of fifteen to eighteen years of age.)

If engineering workshops can be used in boys' schools, why not have nurseries in girls' schools?

In passing, I must refute an objection which will, no doubt, be raised. It will be said: What is the good of arousing in girls a maternal feeling when so many girls will never have children? My reply is: There is no reason why every girl should not have children. We have already seen that the numerical excess of young women over marriageable men is so small as to be negligible—it is certainly not greater than the small proportion of women who do not, in any case, specially desire marriage or children. If our social and educational systems were rightly organised, there is no obstacle to marriage and motherhood for every woman. *It is by preparing girls for celibacy that we make them celibate.*

. . . . .

There is not the slightest doubt that many present-day teachers and parents allow themselves to be influenced by the notion that because a given girl *may* not marry, it is "safer" to prepare her, not only instructionally, but also *emotionally*, for a celibate career.

It is impossible to take up this attitude without inflicting deep injury upon the girl. The adolescent period, as we have seen, is the seed-time of the idealistic and emotional aspects of life, and if it is not utilised for this purpose, emotional starvation and mental arrest will result. The peculiar cynicism of so many modern girls is, no doubt, traceable in large part to the fact that nothing was done to awaken their erotic-idealistic life during the proper period. The libido, in consequence, attached itself to neuter or masculine centres, and the specifically feminine character was arrested. It has been suggested by Dr. Crichton-Miller that the hardness and masculinity of so many girls to-day is a "defence-mechanism." Fundamentally, the girl is afraid of womanhood. No attempt has been made to awaken her erotic nature—a task in which the father should play the first part (especially in the period from fifteen to eighteen)—and she accordingly entrenches herself against the perils of maturity and sex-awakening by developing a truculently independent and quasi-masculine life-outlook.

f. FREEDOM FOR WOMEN

If I were to say that the typical modern girl and young woman is unhappy, restless, discontented, and filled with a vague distress, I should be no more than repeating what she says about herself in her conversation and writings. Almost every book or article written by a modern woman breathes the same spirit of acute dissatisfaction.

It remains to ask: How much of this state of mind is due to a type of education which, as I have sought to show, does not permit a free development of the more fundamental forces of the feminine mind and emotional life? The dissatisfaction is the result of *repression*. In view of the almost unbridled liberty enjoyed by the modern girl, this may seem a somewhat strange statement.

But surely no one supposes that sport, night-club life,

dancing, travel (or even the much-advertised "sexual-freedom"—whatever that may mean!) really correspond to the most permanent and deeply-rooted aspects of womanly psychology? And not for a moment could anyone imagine that, however much a girl may desire to become an engineer, a lawyer, or a racing motorist, this will *of itself* make possible the adequate fulfilment of her personality!

The one thing that most needs doing has been left undone. Modern society has utterly failed to provide women with opportunities for self-fulfilment—the emphasis is upon the word *self*.

In 1914 I visited a family in which there was a little girl, Helen, of ten, and a boy, Jack, a couple of years older. Asking them what they wanted to be when they grew up, the boy said he hoped to be an engineer; the girl replied, without a moment's hesitation: "Oh, I intend to be a mother and have several nice children!"

During the last year I have seen both these again. The boy is an engineer, and doing quite well. His ambition has been realised. But where are the nice children dreamed of by the little girl? Poor Helen is not married; not even engaged to be married. She is not, strange to say, in the least thrilled by the idea of being a chemist, doctor, engineer, or even air-pilot! She is still true to her childhood's desire—"several nice children." The equality of opportunity offered her by the feminists is a complete illusion.

The submission of modern woman to the impersonal technical world-order of the last hundred years, her uncritical acceptance of all its values, her passivity in the face of demands which could have no possible relation to her inner being, has resulted in a disastrous loss of inner freedom and self-confidence, working itself out in a feverish quest of externals.

"Woman is truly less free to-day than ever she has been since time began: in the womanly sense of freedom," wrote D. H. Lawrence in almost the last article to come from his pen.

We are left with the question: How is this freedom to be obtained?

On the one hand, it is impossible to find it through a mere adaptation to an external world-order which has been built up on scientific-technical lines; on the other, it is useless to entertain the idea that woman will ever return to the conditions which obtained before the emancipation. The sole hope of a successful solution lies along the lines indicated by Oskar Schmitz (see p. 164), namely, that "women will, through a realisation of their nature, again desire, of their own free will, to be women, although the possibility of following the opposite path is open to them."

CHAPTER XI

CO-EDUCATION

a. WHAT IS THE AIM?

The earlier sections of this book should have made it abundantly clear that there are deep-seated differences in the psychologies and modes of growth of the two sexes.

If co-education means—as it very often does—that these distinctions are to be too lightly passed over, it is to be condemned. But that does not shut out the possibility of a type of co-educational school in which sufficient attention is paid to the truths of sex psychology. In this case, a mingling of the sexes, within wise limits, may be beneficial. It is unquestionably true that grave evils may result from the segregation of boys or girls—especially in boarding-schools.

Under existing conditions, it is not, I believe, advisable to dogmatise about co-education: in a co-educational school everything depends upon the wisdom and experience of the teachers, upon whether or not they realise adequately the significance of their task and are able to set the right tone. The mere fact that a certain number of boys take their lessons side by side with a certain number of girls is in itself nothing. Speaking generally, the over-enthusiastic belief that some wonderful moral benefit will result from the mere mixing together of boys and girls is no more justified than the opposite conviction that appalling evils will ensue therefrom.

The need for teachers of exceptional insight is, however, to a certain extent an argument against the system, since it will not always, in a given instance, be easy to find the right teachers. Moreover, the organisation of a co-educational school, even supposing the right staff to have been obtained, is a very difficult matter.

Is the head to be a man or a woman? How are the classes to be arranged so that boys from eight or nine onwards come, as we have seen to be so needful, under male influence (for the most part)? How are we to make sure that the girls do not suffer over-strain in competing physically with the boys, or the boys suffer through juxtaposition with girls who are (at the same age) so much more mature? How should we differentiate the curricula at the critical ages?

These are one or two of the rather awkward questions that we must face.

Broadly speaking, it may be said that of recent years there has been a certain reaction against co-education—especially in Germany, Scandinavia, and the United States. It is, however, fair to say that this reaction is directed (in many cases) rather against its existent form than against the idea as such. It has been found, for example, that in the usual type of co-educational school the girls get the worst of it. The school tends to be a boys' school into which girls are squeezed. In America (although not, to any extent, in England or Germany) exceedingly bad moral conditions have frequently resulted.[1]

. . . . .

[1] Lindsey estimates (in Denver) some 700 cases per annum of "sex trouble" amongst girls between 13 and 17 years (half of them attending high-school). 769 cases actually went through the Juvenile Court in two years; 30 pregnancies occurred annually, but a far larger number made successful use of contraceptives. (*The Revolt of Modern Youth*, p. 79.)

Amongst modern books and articles upon co-education, the section on the subject in Dr. F. W. Foerster's *Schule und Charakter* (pub. Schulthess: Zurich) stands out as dealing with fundamental issues in a really penetrating fashion.

It is necessary, says the author, first of all to ask the question: Does the ideal of human progress consist in levelling down the psychic distinctions between men and women, or in preserving and deepening them? Upon the answer our attitude towards the problem of co-education will depend.

For example, the argument is not infrequently used that, through being brought up together with girls, boys become gentler and in general acquire a less markedly masculine disposition, while girls gain in robustness, self-confidence, and activity. Up to a certain point this process may be desirable. But if it be prolonged it would result, logically, in eliminating sex distinction and giving us a race of neuters!

Again, it may be true enough (as often asserted) that constant intercourse causes boys and girls to lose their awkwardness and shyness, and tends to diminish sexual tension.

In both these cases we perceive the assumption (held, perhaps, quite unconsciously) that it is highly desirable to do away with sex difference and attraction as far as is possible. But this is just the point that is open to question!

Why should the modern sex reformer, who almost invariably attacks traditional morality on the ground that it has suppressed sex, be so often a warm advocate of co-education, *precisely on the ground that it tends to weaken the force of sex?* This is one of the many odd contradictions which make up the strange world of illogicality and muddle in which we now live.[1]

Dr. Foerster writes: "Without a doubt we must resist the ideal of levelling down sex differences. The whole wealth of human civilisation rests upon differentiation and individualisation" (p. 59).

This fundamental point of view does not mean that men and women should be one-sidedly masculine and feminine. It is extremely important that the latent femininity in the male and masculinity in the female should be brought to adequate but *not excessive* development. The best men are often those with a streak of the woman in them. And it is true that the old-fashioned, ultra-feminine type of education for girls often produced a weak and sickly sentimentality. It is all a matter of finding the golden mean. Unless we are to produce a state of things that is entirely unwholesome and anti-racial, the male element in the boy and young man should be dominant and the female factors remain in a strictly subordinate position, and the same, in the reverse sense, for the girl (cf. p. 146 footnote).

Whether co-education by itself—i.e. the mere throwing together of young males and females—will help to bring about the right kind of balance of psychological elements is, however, quite another question.

b. THE COMRADESHIP IDEAL

There is a considerable body of opinion in Germany, America, and Scandinavia (some of which is quoted by

[1] Thus Mr. Bertrand (now Lord) Russell explains with enthusiasm that under co-education boys and girls become quite indifferent to sex attraction; but he has himself repeatedly attacked Christianity because, in his view, it has inculcated an indifference to sex!

Dr. Foerster in the work to which I have referred) to the effect that girls in co-educational schools became unduly masculinised. (In England this would hold good to an almost equal extent of girls in separate schools!) It is alleged that on the whole the girls tend to acquire the egoism, self-assertion, and roughness of the boys rather than their best qualities; while the boys do not, to any appreciable extent, develop desirable feminine qualities.

It is clear that a boy, who at the age of, say, twelve to fifteen is passing through a period of plasticity and insecurity, cannot exert any definite influence upon a girl of the same age; he is too much engaged in forming himself to be able to form anyone else.

Foerster says (p. 63): "Boys at the awkward age and half-baked youngsters, whose manhood possesses no ripeness, balance, or security, cannot possibly exert any educative influence over young girls. . . . It is equally impossible for young girls, at an age when they do not yet understand themselves and have not acquired either the strength of purposeful womanhood or the robust self-defence of male youth, to educate the opposite sex. . . ."

On p. 239 of *Die Reifezeit*, Walter Hoffmann writes (in reference to adolescent boys and girls): "Each must first develop his or her own specific character before the attractive power of complementary psychic values can be effective. Therefore, what the young person needs above all, in the period of adolescence, is association with others of the same age and sex. Otherwise the boy is apt to remain soft and the girl to be coarse." He continues (p. 240): "Sexual thoughts are usually absent unless a specially sensual atmosphere dominates the environment, and arouses them prematurely; first and foremost, the social intercourse of boys and girls at these ages is no more than a continuation of the erotic self-absorption stage." The boy, even in seeking the company of girls, is thinking of himself and of the figure he will cut in the eyes of the other boys; while the girl likes to find herself admired.

In Hoffmann's view, even when some sexual aberration takes place, it is usually due to the moral influence of comrades of the same sex rather than to actual sex desire; a girl will often allow herself to be seduced because she wants to have the same experience that friends of hers have had; and a boy will seek to enter into sex relations with a girl because he thinks his friends expect it of him: "It is always a case of problems of *psychic* development."

At this stage the co-educational enthusiast may say: "Yes, but we claim that our system will do away with these erotic reactions and symptoms; the boys will cease to "swank" for the benefit of the girls, and the latter will become good comrades of the boys and not bother about being admired."

This is a very poor argument: as we have seen, this eroticism, with all its crudity, is a most vital stage in the development of youth. To cut it out and pass (or seek to pass) right on to manhood is to impoverish character. The boy who, filled with vague erotic feeling, writes sentimental poetry at the age of sixteen, may live to be a great poet; but if this period were spent in a completely matter-of-fact comradeship with girls, which nipped his emotional stirrings in the bud, his poetical potentialities might remain unstimulated.

Does not the desire to see an entirely "safe" and unsentimental relationship between the sexes during the critical years of adolescence come under the head of "refusal to grow up"? At the back of it is there not the idea: children are innocent, but young men and women are apt to have dangerous emotions, therefore let our children be prevented from becoming men and women! Quite unconsciously this attitude may have a great deal to do with the propaganda in favour of co-education in feminist circles. It is the woman's natural instinct to keep her children young.

It is thoroughly typical of this school of thought to believe that sex instruction of a purely biological kind can take the place of essential womanly characteristics in the girl and manly in the boy. Of chief importance for marriage is mental and emotional maturity. The notion that young people brought up as far as is humanly possible along sexless lines as "good comrades," will achieve ideal relationships through being told all about sex in a bald scientific way is a particularly foolish Utopian dream.

On p. 65 of *Schule und Charakter*, Foerster writes: "It is an illusion that co-education is a specially good preparation for happy marriages. For a truly happy marriage quite another kind of spirit is required than that developed by the close comradely association of adolescents, which always tends, for the sake of the greatest possible common measure of work and sport, to accustom both parties to an *artificial equality* which is anything rather than a preparation for the extraordinary *inequality* of needs and responsibilities of the two sexes in married life. . . . The practice of chivalry, a true respect for women—which can develop only where the differences of sex have not been levelled down, and a full realisation of the deeply-rooted *difference* of the woman; this is a far more appropriate preparation for marriage than the often very naïve and disrespectful familiarity which develops under the co-educational system. . . . [Further] the development of women along masculine lines of self-assertion and independence must, of necessity, result in the suppression of the highest specific qualities of womanhood; but it is these that are the safest guarantees of domestic happiness, for they enable the woman to counter male hardness and egoism with a higher love, instead of merely meeting like with like."

c. SOME PROBLEMS IN CO-EDUCATION

We may now pass on to consider one or two of the special psychological problems which arise.

If we examine a growth-chart for the two sexes (such as is given by Dr. Schneider in his *Schulpraktische Psychologie*, Bd. ii, p. 22, based upon the material of the Institute for Experimental Psychology and Pedagogy in Leipzig) we see that the period of maximum rapidity of growth for the girl is from eleven until fourteen and a half years; and for the boy, from thirteen until seventeen. This is obviously a very important difference, and to give it due weight in the curriculum will not be so easy where there are mixed classes. It would, for example, be unwise for girls of twelve to "make the pace" with boys of anything like the same age, who are not then growing quickly. And, in the opposite sense, it would be bad for boys of sixteen, who are then growing very rapidly indeed, to work parallel with girls who have, at that age, already ceased to develop with maximum speed. At the age of eighteen the girl is nearly if not quite mature, while the boy's growth-curve still rises appreciably: she is often a full-grown woman (with a biological age in relation to the male of about twenty-one) while he has still at least two years of significant development in front of him.

When we have rid ourselves of the idea that age is measured by *years* we perceive much more clearly the real difficulty of co-education. A class of boys and girls of sixteen contains (biologically regarded) boys of sixteen and girls of eighteen to nineteen, in point of relative maturity. Going a little further back, many a girl of fifteen is, in point of sexual and emotional development, on a level with a boy of over eighteen. This is known to every student of human nature. Thus in a mixed class with an average age of fifteen, numbers of boys who are still children find themselves working with girls who are in an entirely different and far more advanced stage of sexual maturity.

The great importance of these considerations will be clear to every educator.

In friendships made in such classes the girl will nearly always prove the dominating partner, and, in a general sense, the girls, by reason of their greater real age, will tend (although in external things often imitating the boys) to impose, in an emotional sense, their personalities upon the less developed boys (this, altogether apart from the more obvious element of sex suggestion, which in America, if not here, has proved to be a very real danger in such schools). On the whole, these points of view strengthen the case for a large degree of segregation for boys.

Yet, for the girls, as will be seen from much of the foregoing, the situation is somewhat different. It is most important that a strong male influence should be experienced in the years (roughly) fourteen to eighteen; and segregation in girls' schools during this period is undesirable (see p. 180). From a psychological standpoint, a mixed staff is of great value for the adolescent girl, and vastly more important than it is for the boy, whose need for female influence comes *earlier* and *later*, rather than during these years.

Summing up the situation, it would appear desirable that boys and girls should spend a part of their school life under co-educational conditions, in so far as these can be united with a full respect for the distinct needs of the two sexes. Perhaps a modified form of co-education would meet the situation, in which classes would be largely separate (and graded with reference to such psychological considerations as we have mentioned), but room would be left for a certain amount of social life in common, and for the employment of a mixed staff—especially for the use of some men teachers on the girls' side. A review of the situation, in the light of modern psychology, would suggest that some arrangement of this kind is the nearest approach to the ideal.

CHAPTER XII

ULTIMATE PROBLEMS

a. THE TRIUMPH OF BOLSHEVISM
b. THE ATTACK ON PERSONALITY
c. THE FAMILY *v.* THE STATE
d. REGRESSION
e. THE ATTACK ON CHRISTIANITY

a. THE TRIUMPH OF BOLSHEVISM

The two recent symposia, *Sex in Civilisation* and *The New Generation* (both published by Messrs. Allen & Unwin), serve very well the purpose of providing for the general reader a review of modern sex-reform tendencies. While some will no doubt find the matter-of-fact rejection of monogamy on the part of nearly all the writers represented rather startling, this will not come as a surprise to those who have followed the latter-day developments of thought on sex matters.

Here is abundant confirmation of Mr. Calverton's remark (to which we have already referred on p. 25) that the Russian Bolshevik ideal of sex morality is now rapidly permeating the whole world. This ideal has already been briefly described. Its essence is the complete abandonment of morality, as we know it in the west (as a definite social norm and religious sanction), and the thoroughgoing *individualisation* of sex. In other words, men and women are to do exactly as they like in their sex life, free from social compulsion or State control. Only where there are children does the State take any interest in the matter. The machinery of quick divorce now functioning in Russia is not, of course, in any essential way different from what used to be called free-love. (Liam O'Flaherty tells us that one of his Russian friends had been "married" fifty times in one year. See footnote to p. 197.) One rather wonders why the State bothers to register marriages at all when they can be dissolved in a couple of minutes the next day. Indeed, visitors to Russia tell us that it now takes much longer to buy a postage stamp than it does to obtain a divorce!

What is perhaps surprising is to find that these extremely revolutionary views—amounting as they do to the absolute negation of western civilisation—should have made the swift progress in the United States which these volumes indicate. When one considers the notorious conservatism of the States in affairs moral and religious, it is certainly remarkable that such a considerable section of educated opinion should be prepared to "go the whole hog" in throwing overboard the entire structure of our moral life. But perhaps it is just because of the rigidity of the prevailing religious life that the reaction comes with such sharpness. It is significant that none of the contributors seems to have any knowledge of progressive Christianity—or indeed of any Christian ideals other than those one might expect to find in the backwoods of Tennessee (or is this deliberate misunderstanding?).

. . . . .

We find here a very striking corroboration of Keyserling's well-known thesis of the fundamental similarity of Russian and American life-ideals. Europe is menaced in its cultural and moral life from the west as well as from the east, and in both cases by forces making for the de-personalisation and crassly materialistic standardisation of life.[1] The ancient European conception of marriage as a union of souls—an ideal which has profoundly influenced civilised thought in spite of the fact that in practice it may seldom have been adequately realised—here gives way to the completely matter-of-fact view of marriage as a mere arrangement of convenience to be terminated immediately it ceases to give satisfaction. There is no reason why the form of sex relationship advocated by modern Russians and Americans should be called marriage at all, since it is in truth an entirely different thing; the name is retained only for the sake of influencing public opinion in favour of the revolution that is proposed. Many a person who would gib at the idea of abolishing marriage and introducing "free-love" can be won over to the idea of "reforming marriage," even when this reform is identical with free-love.

As Keyserling observes (see *America Set Free*, pp. 158ff.), what we here have to deal with is, in both lands, essentially the same thing: it is the reconstitution of life upon a purely animal level. Its philosophical basis is the crudest materialism (of a kind long ago transcended by the progressive thinkers of Europe); its psychology (which is no psychology) is behaviourism;[2] its morality

[1] Cf. also *Christianity and Sex* (Christopher Dawson), p. 6, where, speaking of America and Russia, the author says: "In both the individual is subjected to a ruthless pressure which produces a standardised type of mass-civilisation. . . . We see in both societies the breaking-down of the family as a fixed social unit and the rise of a new type of morality, based upon the complete emancipation of sexual relations from the old social restrictions."

[2] "The behaviouristic method is a kind of inverted anthropomorphism. Under the older animistic auspices, man tended to ascribe to nature in general, including plants and animals, attributes characteristically human. Under the newer animism, the behaviouristic scientist is

in the field of sex is experimental and semi-promiscuous; its economic trend is communistic (in the U.S.A. as well as in Russia);[1] its social system is primitivistic, with a matriarchal tendency.

b. THE ATTACK ON PERSONALITY

The problems of youth, sex, and education under present conditions hinge upon our attitude towards this great world-movement. Is sex education to be given in the interests of monogamy or in the interests of this revolutionary movement? That is the real crux. We have seen (Chap. VII) that when sex instruction is recommended, we need to ask ourselves: Is this to be given as an aid to sexual experiments between young people or is its aim to be preparation for enduring marriage? In the former case, it will be important to explain the technique of sex intercourse, and give instructions in the use of contraceptives; in the latter, the chief emphasis must be laid upon self-control and high ideals of personal and social purity.

Lord Russell says very truly (*Marriage and Morals*, p. 232): "One of the most dangerous fallacies of the conventional moralists is the reduction of sex to the sexual act, in order to be the better able to belabour it. No civilised man and no savage that I have ever heard of is satisfied in his instinct by the bare sexual act. If the

quite content to ascribe to man the characteristics he discovers in animals (preferably white rats)." (Dr. S. D. Schmalhausen, *Sex in Civilisation*, p. 422.)

[1] In spite of the great apparent differences, there are many points of resemblance between the economic system in the U.S.A. (which André Siegfried calls "super-collectivism") and Russian collectivism. (Cf. Keyserling, *America Set Free*, pp. 192 ff.)

impulse which leads to the act is to be satisfied, there must be courtship, there must be love, there must be companionship."

The whole trouble with what we may call the Russian attitude towards sex (whether inside or outside the Soviet Union) is that it is based entirely upon this "reduction of sex," upon the view that *sex is an animal necessity but not a spiritual reality rooted in personality.* It entirely denies love in the idealistic sense. It assumes, like Dr. Watson, that boys and girls and men and women may quite properly meet and mate time and again like so many dogs or cats, with no particular consequences to body or mind. The whole conception of sex amongst the emancipated Russians and Americans is grounded in this de-personalising life philosophy. Men and women are to work together as Robots. Children are to be cared for by the State. Home life is to give way to life in institutions. The common life of man and wife is ruthlessly cut down to a mere coming together for sexual intercourse in their sleeping apartment, just as a couple of dogs might meet behind a bush in the garden. The atmosphere of idealism and romanticism which, however much we may scoff at it in our present mood, has been, and to some extent still is, a very real factor in western life, is here swept away to give place to a bald and unimaginative treatment of sex which leaves it a crude physical act on the level of eating and drinking.[1]

[1] Those who feel inclined to doubt this statement should read *Humanity Uprooted*, by Maurice Hindus, where a lucid account is given of the materialisation of sex in modern Russia by one who is not an anti-Bolshevik. Liam O'Flaherty's *I Went to Russia* is interesting, too, in this connection.

Speaking of certain "Bolshevised" upper-class circles in England, Aldous Huxley writes: "In so far as they are sexual and emotional beings, the youngest of our contemporaries seem to be entirely

In order to understand this movement of "reduction" we may best regard it as a phase—perhaps the end-phase—of the mechanical-technical life-outlook of the last two or three generations in the west. It is the product not of a special broad-mindedness (as its promoters believe) but of a quite unprecedented narrowness of concentration upon a single aspect of life. Like the Marxian view of history, it impresses by its entire singleness its freedom from all that transcends the immediate range of a mediocre intellect. But like the materialistic philosophy of history, its simplicity and unity are utterly misleading. Only by leaving out of account absolutely vital realities is it possible to present this childishly over-simplified picture of human sex life.

In reading many of the contributions in these symposia one is driven to smile at the crass type of mentality which can really believe that the application of a little science is all that is needed to solve our sexual troubles: some matter-of-fact instruction, the removal of restrictions on the free social intercourse of the sexes, a few lessons in the technique of sexual intercourse, and the use of contraceptives—and there you are! The conflicts of adolescence will disappear, the need for tiresome self-control will cease to exist, there will be no more worries about the untimely arrival of babies, the divorce problem will be solved—and so on. The integrity of personality, the

uncivilised. And they admit their savagery in these matters, they abandon themselves to it. 'Savagery' is perhaps the wrong word; for savages are co-ordinated within a rigid framework of taboos. Our modern savages have no taboos of any sort. They copulate with the casual promiscuity of dogs; they make use of every violent emotion-producing sensation for its own sake, because it gives a momentary thrill. . . . They pass from state to mental state with the enjoyment of children visiting the side-shows of a fair." (*Proper Studies*, p. 259.)

mystery of sex, the sacredness of love, the holiness of motherhood, the reverence for parenthood—all these things, which used to mean so much, are nothing but "hocus-pocus" or "bunk" (to quote terms employed by several of the contributors).

. . . . .

Writing thus, I do not for a moment suggest that all was well in the age we have just passed through. A reaction against Victorian Puritanism was overdue. Even from the standpoint of orthodoxy such a reaction represents a return to views of sex held in earlier and saner ages. The hostility between religion and sex is a comparatively new development (apart from ascetic movements). When St. Catherine of Thüringia rejoined her husband after a lengthy separation it is recorded that she kissed him for eighteen hours without ceasing. And St. Augustine held that sexual intercourse was a thing as healthy and good as the desire for food and drink. (See *Christianity and Sex* by Christopher Dawson, p. 12.) (This for the benefit of those who take their ideas of traditional teaching from tendencious modern publications!)

A restoration of sex to the position of vital importance which it should occupy in a healthy civilisation is one thing; but a cult of sex as an amusement, divorced from ethical and aesthetic values and sterilised by contraceptives (reduced, in fact, to *unimportance* by being made essentially trivial) is quite another! Those who imagine that the neo-pagan sex revival in Anglo-Saxondom is a return to nature and "wholesomeness" have missed the point of the whole matter. It is an essentially artificial, mechanised, and de-vitalised form of sex life which is here offered, as a peculiarly "titivating" form of amusement, to the jaded rich boys and girls of a decaying plutocracy.

The situation created in Russia ("the land without love") through the degradation of sex to the level of a needful act of physical well-being, devoid of personal values or ethical significance, is essentially quite similar to that in emancipated America, even if, under the hammer and sickle, there is no mass-produced eroticism, with jazz and rye whisky accompaniment. The *devaluation of sex* in a world devoted to business and "efficiency" is in both cases the central fact.

If we reject the modern pseudo-pagan sex movement (a vastly different matter from real paganism, which imparted dignity and meaning to sex), this must not be taken to mean that we should remain satisfied with the impoverished ideals of the Victorian age. My whole point is that it is essential to press beyond both the Puritan distortion of religion and the unthinking and crudely emotional reaction against it, before we can find a genuine basis for a new and truer valuation of sex in the modern world. But we shall be deceiving ourselves if we think that the excesses of a shallow and immature sexuality will not be several degrees worse than the régime of Mrs. Grundy!

c. THE FAMILY *v.* THE STATE

To sum up: personality, individual life, the family (and the whole realm of ethical relationships bound up with it) are all in process of being sacrificed upon the altar of the all-powerful mechanical State. Mass-life, after the Russian ideal, is to swallow up the ego (already undermined by modern science, and especially by behaviouristic psychology). Sex remains, not as a real factor, because no values must be left powerful enough to challenge the sole reality—the State, but as a means of amusement to pass the time while the worker is not making tractors for the Five Year Plan or producing automobiles for an American syndicate. The entire movement signifies the abandonment of the personalistic cultural ideals of Europe (which rest upon the family) and the return to an undifferentiated mass-life of pre-Socratic type.

To those who look at this tendency superficially it may well seem that the destruction of the family will pave the way for a richer personal life. In reality, as we shall see later, the elimination of personal ties (which possess definite ethical value) merely results in the forging of ties of another kind—namely, those which bind the individual to the State. The cry "Down with the Family" does not proclaim a life of freedom; on the contrary, it is invariably accompanied by complete prostration before the altar of the State (cf. p. 167, footnote). This is in fact *necessary*.

Atomistic individualism (which denies all moral relationships between man and woman, parent and child, and dissolves all positive standards) is just the very thing which compels the intervention of the State. *Something* must be done to create social unity, and if this unity does not exist in the social ethic of the people, it must be imposed forcibly by the State.

It is, in addition, obvious that the whole trend of present-day economic life is to destroy family relationships and substitute for them dependence upon the State or upon State-controlled trusts and syndicates.

In this way modern society tends, more and more, to become a congregation of atoms, entirely isolated in a moral sense, but rigidly bound together through their subjection to the State.

. . . . .

It was Olive Schreiner (in *Woman and Labour*) who pointed out so forcibly how the modern economic system has undermined the family by taking away from the home and transferring to the factory nearly all the activities that once made home life the centre of human interest. Of late, this movement away from the home extends even to the education of very young children, and all the truly "advanced" now believe that babies of two (or even one-and-a-half) should not be allowed to remain at home; and there is a newer and still more "advanced" school which does not consider it right that babies should ever know their parents at all—they should be reared from birth by the State! In this way, it is clear, the home is gradually deprived, by processes which (in the economic field, at least) we are apparently quite powerless to avert, of every vestige of *raison d'être*; it becomes a mere sleeping apartment. That this process will go further and further—given modern conditions—is quite inevitable.

In the Anglo-Saxon lands especially, feminism has, from the beginning, encouraged this home-destroying process. In Olive Schreiner's view, woman had no alternative but to follow her occupations into the factory and leave the home to perish; and the modern woman's movement has continued to develop along the lines laid down by the authoress of *Woman and Labour*. We thus witness the odd paradox that, although most women still love the home and desire home-life, the women's movement as an organised force is one of the strongest factors working for the destruction of the home. The egocentric ideology of the movement compels it to lend support to every tendency which makes women independent by carrying them away from the home, and to all those forces which create separate interests as between husband and wife. And as we have seen in another place (Chap. X), it invariably urges for girls an education unfitting them for home-life, and brands as "reactionaries" all those who think that girls should receive a training with a view to marriage.

A classical document of the modern woman's movement, in its bearing upon the family, is *Marriage in the New World* (contained in Keyserling's symposium, *Marriage*), by Dr. Beatrice Hinkle, one of New York's leading women doctors, from which I take the following typical passage:

"Woman's struggle to-day is the mighty birth-throes of a new self. The cult of the ego which dominates this age has produced its effect upon her, and she is becoming articulate and thinking—she is demanding recognition for herself as an individual, separate and distinct from man. Man and woman have become "two distinct personalities," "the twain are no longer one flesh."

Here we have, in a nutshell, the marriage problem of to-day. The meaning of marriage is the union of two personalities. Behind it lies the belief that neither of these two would have attained to their fullest development had they remained in separate distinctness. This quotation (as is indeed clear enough from the rest of the article) means something quite other than the freeing of woman from subjection. It implies a view of marriage that is the flat negation of the Christian view, and an acceptance of Bolshevist ideals. It rests upon the entirely false assumption that each separate individual is a complete whole, and will best develop in the fullest possible isolation. Like the whole literature of feminism, *it denies the bi-polarity of humanity*. But woman is not, in reality, an individual separate and distinct from man. She is one half of the race, inseparably linked, for good or evil, with the other half, and fundamentally incapable (much more, even, than man) of achieving salvation through self-centred detachment.

Dr. Hinkle herself admits, with admirable candour, that the practical results of the new individualism are destructive, that marriage is thus made immeasurably more difficult. But it is her belief that there can be no going back; the only way is forward through an ever-increasing individualism until at last the stage is reached when fully emancipated separate personalities have evolved a free ethic. The old ideals of woman's duty to society and the family are "gone, never to return."

Assuredly no one to-day is going to deny woman's right to become "articulate and thinking." But what we have here is a totally false position of the problem. On the one hand lies (it is implied) subjection and no thinking; on the other, thinking and emancipation through separation and the disruption of the family. The assumption that when women think they will at once perceive their complete separateness from men is simply ludicrous.

I have dwelt upon Dr. Hinkle's contribution because it is thoroughly typical. Virtually all recent works dealing with the family are mere re-statements of the same *Lebensanschauung*. Thus, in *Halcyon* (a recent book by one of the acknowledged leaders of English feminism) we find the same questions answered in the same way. The goal is always complete ego-centricity, and the argument is always based on the assumption that this self-development will be fatally hampered by positive social ties, *although not by subjection to the impersonal State!*[1]

. . . . .

It is, of course, perfectly true (as we saw in Chap. I) that millions of people take no notice of these "advanced" ideas. They continue to live, work, marry, and bring up children. *But these millions are inarticulate.* They are entirely without influence upon the course of events. On the other hand, the circles that *are self-conscious and artistically and intellectually creative* are saturated through and through with the "cult of the ego," and from them the influence percolates downwards until it reaches, in one form or another, every stratum of the national life. To-day, thanks largely to the ubiquitous cinema, there is scarcely a boy or girl in the remotest village who has not caught some hint of the new gospel of individualism and erotic liberty. If the Churches are powerless to work against this influence, it is not least because they are themselves deeply permeated, in varying degrees, with the same doctrines.

The new life-outlook is coming increasingly to dominate our social legislation. We are now compelled to face the fact that the western State is closely allied with the forces which attack the family.

The decay of the family brings with it certain evils (for example, the underfeeding of young children or the

[1] Cf. the typical feminist view in the footnote to p. 167.

neglect of maternity). At once there is a call for State action. The State accordingly takes over these functions from the family, and the latter is automatically rendered superfluous. The best way to destroy a social institution is to supplant it. Year by year the State advances further and further into the field of the ever-weakening family. We see this going on, but we cannot stop it.[1]

The system of Family Allowances (should it be introduced) will be another nail in the coffin of the family, because it marks a yet more advanced stage in the assumption by the State of parental function. It would, of course, greatly reduce the interest of the father (especially) in his offspring, for it tends to make him superfluous.

It is certain, too, that this measure will scarcely be upon the Statute Book before an agitation will begin on behalf of illegitimate children. In a couple of years (at most) they will be placed on a level with legitimate children—for who can resist an appeal on behalf of innocent children? It will then make little or no difference, economically, to a woman of the poorer classes whether she has a husband or not. The children will be the joint property of the mother and the State, *after the style of the primitive matriarchies*. Once this were accomplished "the family would probably cease, after a time, to be bi-parental, the father being of no more importance than among cats and dogs." (Bertrand Russell, *ibid*., p. 168.)

[1] Even a thinker like Bertrand Russell, who certainly cannot be accused of reactionary sympathies, views the impending extinction of the family with alarm. On p. 162 of his recent work, *Marriage and Morals*, he writes: "Although the law means to uphold the family, it has in modern times increasingly intervened between parents and children, and is gradually becoming, against the wish and intention of law-makers, one of the chief engines for the break-up of the family system."

It was upon the cultural level of primitive naturalism and mass-life that the matriarchy arose, and as we are now returning (*via* science and the Russo-American movement) to another, more sophisticated naturalism, which rejects *Geist* and personality not from ignorance, but from supposed knowledge, it is not, after all, very extraordinary that the moral life of the age shows a marked tendency to follow the lines it took in the days prior to European culture.

d. REGRESSION

In the introduction to Mr. Calverton's *The Bankruptcy of Marriage*, Mr. Briffault (author of *The Mothers*) expresses the opinion that the tendency of modern social life is irresistibly in the direction of a form of matriarchy.

There is no doubt that such a statement arouses scepticism in the mind of the man in the street. As he sees it we are drawing nearer to sex equality. In reality, the matter is not so simple.

The crumbling away of the patriarchal order might, *theoretically*, lead to a state of sex equality. But in practice, when the family is atomised the mother becomes the guardian of the children and the rights tend to centre in her. We revert to a more primitive social form.

In Chapter VIII a very definite example has been given of how the formal and abstract notion of sex equality, derived from rationalism, leads, in practice, to inequality favouring the woman. This is quite typical of what is happening in all the western lands. The woman is admitted on (more or less) equal terms to masculine rights and privileges; but, at the same time, she retains the sheltered position derived from her ancient status of protection.

The reformers of the last century supposed, like good, old, simple-minded theorists, that when women acquired the same rights and privileges as men they would at once hasten to surrender their sex privileges. But time passes by, and we do not notice any inclination on the part either of ordinary women or of feminist politicians to give up anything of their feminine privileges.[1] But if these privileges are not *voluntarily* surrendered by women, it is clear that women are gradually acquiring a favoured and even dominant position. With regard to any compulsion upon women, this is obviously out of the question, since no politician could possibly afford to risk popularity and votes by bringing forward legislation establishing sex equality to the disadvantage of women! The woman's cause is to-day the popular cause *with both sexes*. Of this there cannot be the slightest doubt.

The reason for this is already known to the reader. In the first section of this study we saw how "the modern spirit" represents precisely feminine as opposed to masculine values. Psychological factors thus conspire with economic to place woman in a leading position. To-day everyone laughs at the husband who talks of his rights; but no one sees anything amusing in the wife's demand for rights: her case is regarded as a serious

[1] For example, in an age when thousands of women earn as good money, or better, than a man, the husband of a wife who lives separated from him is still expected to maintain her, just as if she were the helpless creature of eighty years ago. Again, while immense efforts have been made to secure for married women the right of entry into every field of work, no move has been made to liberate husbands from their family liabilities. Even when the wife's income is larger than that of the husband, it is he and he alone who is liable for the upkeep of the family.

social problem. The most striking feature of the whole situation is the instinctive bias of the general public. A recent attempt to start a league for men's rights was instantly killed by laughter, but nobody could have said why they laughed. Perhaps it was because of a subconscious realisation of the truth of Keyserling's words, "the new-emerging moral code is that of a decisively Amazonian world" (*Europe*, p. 68).[1]

. . . . .

The whole situation is confused and obscured by the use of the phrase "sex equality" in a totally undefined sense. The man in the street no doubt believes that it means an identical legal and social standing for men and women. Yet, apparently, this is exactly what it does *not* mean when employed by politicians.

[1] The spread of this code is closely associated with the progressive Americanisation of the western world. Mr. Hewitt-Myring, a very competent observer, wrote in the *Daily News* of November 1, 1928, that the United States is saturated with a belief in the "essential superiority of the female," who now "gets it both ways"; she is placed on a level with the male, on the grounds of equality, and elevated above him on the grounds of femininity. It thus follows that the woman occupies a position that is definitely superior to that of the man, both legally and socially. Nevertheless, in the writer's opinion, the "dominant woman" is less happy than the "enchained male."

The well-known German writer, Adolf Halfeld, writes (*Amerika und der Amerikanismus*, p. 219): "The American not only permits the social, legal, and cultural supremacy of women; he is convinced that it is necessary. He thinks in real earnest that woman is morally, aesthetically, and intellectually his superior, and that this is a state of things ordained by nature."

In *America Set Free*, Count Keyserling is equally emphatic, and we read on p. 308: "If all men in America are supposed to be equal, every American man instinctively admits—if not in his thoughts and words then all the more in his attitude and in his actions—that woman represents a higher state of being than he does. Women actually represent a higher caste in the United States."

In a recent debate with a well-known feminist and ardent advocate of "sex equality," I asked her the plain question: "Would you be willing to accept a complete equalisation of the law as between men and women, involving (as of course it would) the liberation of the husband from all legal liabilities not shared equally by the wife?" She replied at once: "No, that is impossible, because women need special legislation to protect their interests as wives and mothers." In other words, her demand was not for equality at all but for a state of society in which women would get-it-both-ways—benefit by "equality" when it was a question of entering into any male career or occupation, and by inequality when it was a matter of their special sex interests.

The extraordinary muddle which now exists with regard to the whole question of sex equality was illustrated in a striking way in the discussion of the sex-equality problem carried on in the columns of the *Daily News* (in February 1929), when several leading feminists and certain opponents put their views before the public.

Mrs. Maud Crofts (author of *Women under English Law*), who may be regarded as one of the chief spokeswomen of the moderate feminists, dealt in considerable detail with the privileges problem, and made it clear that an abandonment of the more basic privileges was out of the question: "These must survive," she wrote, "owing to the different duties and functions of the majority of men and women." Precisely. *The opponents of sex equality have always said that men and women have different functions*. There could be no better illustration of the modern sex reversal than the fact that this time-worn phrase is now being used by feminists as an argument against a complete and logical sex equality. The true and proper corollary of Mrs. Crofts' position would be that *men, like women, should receive certain privileges corresponding to their specific functional needs*—for example, if a married man is still to be held legally responsible for his wife and family (as she maintains), he must, in justice, receive a higher professional remuneration than that granted to a woman, either single or married, since she is free from these special legal burdens. This must be transparently obvious to any fair-minded person.[1]

I must repeat that while it might be possible, in a reorganised society based upon rational principles, to abolish *all* sex privilege and establish true equality, there is not, in the Anglo-Saxon lands, any likelihood of such a development. As I sought to show in my study *Woman and Society*, what is actually occurring in the modern western world is a steady drift in the direction of American conditions. Even in Spain, a land not specially exposed to these influences, the new legislation intro-

[1] Another representative feminist puts the position even more uncompromisingly. Miss Nancy Stewart Parnell, who is widely known in the North of England as a woman speaker, wrote (in the *Daily News* of February 11, 1929) that the married woman "demands as a right, and not as a privilege, a different status in the eyes of the law and of society from either men or her unmarried sisters." This is getting worse and worse. The privileges have now become rights! Here we have the definite statement that women demand as a right a different and privileged status. And this after years of agitation in which women have repeated until we were tired of hearing it that what they were fighting for was *equality* of legal status! How precisely we are reminded of the arguments of my childhood days, when the boot was on the other leg. I can remember sitting on a footstool in my mother's drawing-room and hearing men say that women could not be admitted to equal rights because men, as soldiers and fathers of families and so on, must have their peculiar sex privileges. For fathers, read mothers, and for soldiers, read wives, and there is your sex reversal! The wheel has almost completed a full revolution.

duced by the revolutionary party does not establish sex equality (in spite of the original intention that it should) but, in marriage laws, places the woman in the leading position.

In the new Russia, Mr. Calverton tells us (*Sex in Civilisation*, p. 276) that, although the revolution proclaimed sex equality, the laws with regard to moral questions have been "invariably designed" in the interests of women rather than men; and indeed this is clear enough when we know that in the case of illegitimate children the rights are vested in the mother and the duties in the father. A man with illegitimate children is ruined; but the mother of two or three such soon finds herself in a good position, especially if the fathers are fairly well-to-do—since she can claim on each child a share of the father's income. When we remember further that men are frequently called upon to pay paternity allowances on behalf of children which they did not beget, we begin to realise what "sex equality" means under such conditions!

• • • • •

It would clearly be impossible to develop further this important theme within these narrow limits, but enough has been said to indicate that the general trend of modern life towards a new matriarchy is not quite so fantastic as those who live in the thought-world of pre-war days might suppose. There is, indeed, a sort of necessity about the process. The more the family weakens, the more it becomes centred in the mother as the sole stable personality. Already, in America, one meets women with a collection of children from diverse fathers (as in the novels of Edith Wharton)[1], and this kind of family is quite openly the goal of advanced feminists in this country.

This trend constitutes, from the standpoint of this study, a *regression*. It means the abandonment of both monogamy and sex equality, two of the highest ideals of western life, and a backward movement to the mass-life, which marks a lower type of society than the differentiated personalism of the European tradition. It would be an error to imagine that because those who come forward openly to advocate revolutionary changes in morals have no great influence in Great Britain, we can therefore afford to treat the situation lightly. The whole point of my argument is that the underlying forces now moving western life, and impelling all parties —*the most conservative as well as the "left-wingers"*— are making irresistibly in the direction of a complete system of State control, involving the gradual destruction of the family and the realisation of a social system after impersonal mass-ideals. It is the ego-centric ideology now basic in western civilisation which, by dissolving all bonds other than those imposed by the State, atomises society and automatically reduces it to an amorphous mass.

Since the family lies at the very heart of the whole system of western civilisation, the problems dealt with in this section if, in seeming, not always closely related to Youth, are in truth at the very root of the whole matter. The attitude of the rising generation towards the problems of the family, marriage, and sex will be profoundly determinative of our future.

[1] In the report of a recent English Society wedding it was stated that the bride was accompanied by two of her children "by one of her former husbands."

e. THE ATTACK ON CHRISTIANITY

Christianity is regarded as, in a very special sense, "the enemy" by the regressionists, in view of its position as the chief defender of personality, free-will, the family, monogamy, and the ego against the mass. All these things "hang together" and they all form a part of the problem of Youth and Sex if we regard it in the light of ultimate values.

The two symposia referred to on p. 193 will do as well as any other publications to illustrate this attack upon religion. Most of the numerous references to Christianity in these two volumes might have come direct from the propaganda department of the Soviet Union. If any reader of these works were to take at their face-value the statements made, he would find himself believing that Christians as a body are hostile to every form of sex life; that happy marriages between persons belonging to Christian bodies are entirely unknown; that in the Catholic lands (such as Spain or Italy) the people have no natural sex life whatever; that no Christian has ever written any great literature of sex; that (since Christianity is again and again alleged to be "the enemy of life") the birth-rate amongst Christians is much lower than amongst non-Christians—and a number of other quite fantastic things.

We are given long strings of extracts—carefully selected—from early Christian writers of an ultra-ascetic turn, but it is not made clear that this sort of teaching has never been the basis of the doctrine of the Churches, either Catholic or Protestant. In the Catholic Church, as is well known, the ascetic life is never urged upon those who do not feel a special call to it.

As a psychological study of intellectuals working-off their repressions these contributions are of considerable interest, but as scientific contributions to the matter in question they are entirely unreliable.

There is a complete absence of what the Germans call *Abgeklärtheit*, the inward clarification of the mind. And for this reason these hysterical diatribes against religion and morality fail to convince. Their writers do not really know what they mean. As their attitude is predominantly emotional and, like other "moderns," they have a hearty contempt for reason, they constantly find themselves entangled in rather amusing contradictions.

For example, the main burden of Mr. Briffault's complaint is that Christianity imposes taboos upon sex life which cause harmful repression and a stifling of instinct. (See *The New Generation*, p. 680.) Yet on p. 693 of the same article we find him calmly stating that Christianity has "fanned the embers [of sex instinct] into a lively flame." Since it is clear that Mr. Briffault (quite rightly) regards sex instinct as highly desirable, this fanning process ought to be after his own heart! Does he think sex ought not to be a lively flame? In reality, as is perfectly obvious, he thinks any stick is good enough with which to beat Christianity. First we are told that sex is killed by Christianity; then that it is unduly stimulated!

On the same page (693) Mr. Briffault informs us, with admiration, that "primitive man regards sex with comparative calm." Just so. His sex feeling is not developed. It has not been fanned into flame. This admission only goes to make confusion worse confounded. Here Mr. Briffault takes sides, so to speak, with the primitive man against the Christian, on the ground that the former is less highly sexed than the latter, and yet the whole point of his bitter attack on Christianity is that it reduces the force of sex!

But does anyone attach much weight to the views upon religion of a writer who can speak of "the Christian plan of suppressing sex root and branch" (p. 692) and "the Christian plan of abolishing sex"? (p. 693). An hour spent in looking up the teaching of the Catholic Church (or of any of the leading Protestant bodies) would have made impossible such wild statements as these.[1]

If Mr. Briffault and his allies had taken the pains to make a sincere study of authoritative Christian writers, they would have discovered to their surprise that the Catholic Church, at least (which has never lacked sound psychological insight), has all along been perfectly aware of the fact that the limitation (not suppression)

[1] As an example of modern Christian opinion, I may quote from an address recently given by the Archbishop of York (as reported in *The Church Times*, February 27, 1931):

". . . it is not possible for any Christian to say that anything that God made is inherently evil . . . when St. John wanted to make his great proclamation he did not say, 'the Word became man'; he deliberately took the word which represents the lowest elements in human nature, and said, 'the Word became flesh.' " We have to recognise (said the Archbishop) "the complete wholesomeness of the natural fact of sex," but, according to the Christian view, this goes hand in hand with monogamy, for sex should be "the expression of a spiritual union of such a quality that it is inevitably life-long."

It may be added that this is precisely the view of sex proclaimed by St. Augustine and St. Thomas Aquinas. Christopher Dawson writes (*Progress and Religion*, p. 247): "Christianity . . . has always resisted the Gnostic or Manichaean tendency to regard the material world as intrinsically evil. It seeks not the destruction of nature, or the negation of nature, but its spiritualisation and its incorporation in a higher order of reality."

of sex has the effect of increasing the power of sex instinct and thus has a definite biological value.[1]

If anything were lacking to make complete the confusion of mind amongst typical "moderns" on all these matters, it is to be found in their attitude towards this problem of the biological urge.

On p. 257 of *Sex and Civilisation*, Mr. Calverton (who speaks for a large body of "moderns") declares that Christians still regard sex as "wholly evil" because it perpetuates life! Yet a host of other writers in the same camp make it a chief charge against Christianity that it encourages a high birth-rate, and are themselves greatly disturbed at the idea that sex should be used to perpetuate life (cf., for example, Mrs. Sanger's article in this same volume). What a muddle! Mr. X. or Professor Y. is quite capable of stating on one page that "religion destroys life," and on the next that bishops are "reactionaries" because they advocate a high birth-rate. These ludicrous inconsistencies are in more than one way very significant; they illustrate both the lack of inner clarity in the modern movement and the almost incredibly uncritical mentality of those who consume this sort of muddle-headed literature.

Even Bertrand Russell, who is a logician, finds it impossible to keep his head clear when he sees the red rag of Christianity before his eyes. On p. 83 of his recent

[1] Cf. Freud, *Collected Papers*, vol. iv, p. 214: "The value the mind sets on erotic needs instantly sinks as soon as the satisfaction becomes readily obtainable. Some obstacle is necessary to swell the tide of the libido to its height—the ascetic tendency of Christianity had the effect of raising the psychical value of love in a way that heathen antiquity could never achieve." (Quoted by Roback on p. 151 of *Sex and Civilisation*.) This is a special aspect of that general need for conflict, implied in psycho-analysis, and referred to on p. 116.

work, *Marriage and Morals*, he tells us that the "hush-hush" attitude towards sex leads to a hampering of curiosity in the young; "if it be wicked to ask how babies are made, it may, for aught the child can tell, be equally wicked to ask how aeroplanes are made." To our considerable astonishment we then find him explaining on p. 85 (only two pages on) that if we make a mystery of sex it "enormously increases the natural curiosity of the young on the subject." This is all very curious. Bertrand Russell knows very well that sex curiosity and general curiosity are closely related; he tells us how valuable it is to keep curiosity alive; he then goes on to denounce those who increase curiosity; and concludes by arguing as if the killing of curiosity in the young were a most desirable aim! The author of *Marriage and Morals* seems to be in the same boat with Mr. Briffault; he cannot quite decide whether it will pay him best to attack Christianity for the harm it has done by deadening sex feeling and curiosity about sex, or because it has unduly stimulated the sexual side of life—so, like a true "modern," he makes both accusations at once and they cancel one another out.

Another most entertaining example of "the modern spirit" is to be found in *Marriage and Morals*, where the author, after devoting a large amount of space to an eloquent argument in favour of freedom in love and maternity and denouncing the wrongfulness of controlling by authority what should be a pure expression of personal feeling, suddenly turns completely round, and (in chap. xvii) tells us how an international government should control maternity (if necessary, even by force) in the interests of the systematic regulation of population. In other words, although the right of maternity is sacred and free, if a young woman should have the misfortune to belong to a State with an increasing population, she should be compelled by law to remain sterile. This international tribunal is (apparently) to enforce sterility upon millions of women, without their having any choice in the matter at all; yet celibacy in religious life (which is voluntary) is one of this distinguished propagandist's chief abhorrences! It is a fairly safe principle that the more the "emancipated" proclaim the freedom of the individual, the more they are willing to put all power into the hands of the State machine; what they give with one hand they take away with the other!

. . . . .

These examples are of some importance because they illustrate a persistent tendency, traceable right through nearly all present-day literature of the type we are considering. It is assumed that under free conditions, where there are no taboos and restrictions, sex will develop to its finest flower, and a special attack is directed against Christianity on the ground that it represses sex. Yet at the same time it is realised (largely through the study of savage tribes) that sex is much less intense when it "spreads itself" than when it is confined to definite, narrow channels. This at once suggests the possibility of dealing the detested Christians another whack on the other cheek, and they are now accused of increasing the intensity of sex by preventing it "spreading itself."

Enough has been said to indicate very plainly the chaotic condition of our modern thought in the field of values—moral and intellectual. Yet, without some adequate solution to these ultimate problems, it must remain impossible for us to find any clear path in relation to the more limited problems raised in this study. The whole life and development of youth is inseparably bound up with the question: Where are we going?

INDEX